" The Ol[...]
to mag[...]
and an[...]
politica[...] ...u popular mythology.
Filled with fascinating details and conveyed in sharp,
accessible prose, the books make the everyday world
come to life. Be warned: once you've read a few of these,
you'll start walking around your house, picking up
random objects, and musing aloud: 'I wonder what the
story is behind this thing?'"

Steven Johnson, author of *Where Good Ideas*
Come From and *How We Got to Now*

" Object Lessons describes themselves as 'short, beautiful
books,' and to that, I'll say, amen. . . . If you read enough
Object Lessons books, you'll fill your head with plenty
of trivia to amaze and annoy your friends and loved
ones—caution recommended on pontificating on the
objects surrounding you. More importantly, though
. . . they inspire us to take a second look at parts of
the everyday that we've taken for granted. These are
not so much lessons about the objects themselves,
but opportunities for self-reflection and storytelling.
They remind us that we are surrounded by a wondrous
world, as long as we care to look."

John Warner, *The Chicago Tribune*

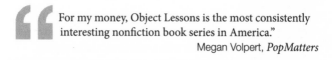

For my money, Object Lessons is the most consistently interesting nonfiction book series in America."

Megan Volpert, *PopMatters*

Besides being beautiful little hand-sized objects themselves, showcasing exceptional writing, the wonder of these books is that they exist at all . . . Uniformly excellent, engaging, thought-provoking, and informative."

Jennifer Bort Yacovissi, *Washington Independent Review of Books*

. . . edifying and entertaining . . . perfect for slipping in a pocket and pulling out when life is on hold."

Sarah Murdoch, *Toronto Star*

[W]itty, thought-provoking, and poetic . . . These little books are a page-flipper's dream."

John Timpane, *The Philadelphia Inquirer*

Though short, at roughly 25,000 words apiece, these books are anything but slight."

Marina Benjamin, *New Statesman*

> The joy of the series, of reading *Remote Control, Golf Ball, Driver's License, Drone, Silence, Glass, Refrigerator, Hotel,* and *Waste* . . . in quick succession, lies in encountering the various turns through which each of their authors has been put by his or her object. . . . The object predominates, sits squarely center stage, directs the action. The object decides the genre, the chronology, and the limits of the study. Accordingly, the author has to take her cue from the *thing* she chose or that chose her. The result is a wonderfully uneven series of books, each one a *thing* unto itself."
>
> Julian Yates, *Los Angeles Review of Books*

> The Object Lessons series has a beautifully simple premise. Each book or essay centers on a specific object. This can be mundane or unexpected, humorous or politically timely. Whatever the subject, these descriptions reveal the rich worlds hidden under the surface of things."
>
> Christine Ro, *Book Riot*

> . . . a sensibility somewhere between Roland Barthes and Wes Anderson."
>
> Simon Reynolds, author of *Retromania: Pop Culture's Addiction to Its Own Past*

OBJECT LESSONS

A book series about the hidden lives of ordinary things.

Series Editors:

Ian Bogost and Christopher Schaberg

reveals how the objects society
encourages us to play w/ ·
as girls shape the women
we become

In association with

LOYOLA UNIVERSITY NEW ORLEANS   Washington University in St. Louis

BOOKS IN THE SERIES

Bird by Erik Anderson
Blackface by Ayanna Thompson
Blanket by Kara Thompson
Bookshelf by Lydia Pyne
Bread by Scott Cutler Shershow
Bulletproof Vest by Kenneth R. Rosen
Burger by Carol J. Adams
Cell Tower by Steven E. Jones
Cigarette Lighter by Jack Pendarvis
Coffee by Dinah Lenney
Compact Disc by Robert Barry
Doctor by Andrew Bomback
Doll Maria Teresa Hart
Driver's License by Meredith Castile
Drone by Adam Rothstein
Dust by Michael Marder
Earth by Jeffrey Jerome Cohen and Linda T. Elkins-Tanton
Egg by Nicole Walker
Email by Randy Malamud
Environment by Rolf Halden
Exit by Laura Waddell
Eye Chart by William Germano
Fake by Kati Stevens
Fat by Hanne Blank
Football by Mark Yakich
Glass by John Garrison
Golf Ball by Harry Brown
Gin by Shonna Milliken Humphrey
Glitter by Nicole Seymour
Hair by Scott Lowe
Hashtag by Elizabeth Losh
High Heel by Summer Brennan
Hood by Alison Kinney
Hotel by Joanna Walsh
Hyphen by Pardis Mahdavi
Jet Lag by Christopher J. Lee
Luggage by Susan Harlan
Magnet by Eva Barbarossa
Ocean by Steve Mentz
Office by Sheila Liming
Password by Martin Paul Eve
Perfume by Megan Volpert
Personal Stereo by Rebecca Tuhus-Dubrow
Phone Booth by Ariana Kelly
Pill by Robert Bennett
Political Sign by Tobias Carroll
Potato by Rebecca Earle
Questionnaire by Evan Kindley
Recipe by Lynn Z. Bloom
Refrigerator by Jonathan Rees
Remote Control by Caetlin Benson-Allott
Rust by Jean-Michel Rabaté
Sewer by Jessica Leigh Hester
Shipping Container by Craig Martin
Shopping Mall by Matthew Newton
Signature by Hunter Dukes
Silence by John Biguenet
Skateboard by Jonathan Russell Clark
Snake by Erica Wright
Sock by Kim Adrian
Souvenir by Rolf Potts
Spacecraft by Timothy Morton
Sticker by Henry Hoke
Stroller by Amanda Parrish Morgan
Traffic by Paul Josephson
Tree by Matthew Battles
Trench Coat by Jane Tynan
Tumor by Anna Leahy
TV by Susan Bordo
Veil by Rafia Zakaria
Waste by Brian Thill
Whale Song by Margret Grebowicz
Air Conditioning by Hsuan L. Hsu (Forthcoming)
Alarm by Alice Bennett (Forthcoming)
Bicycle by Jonathan Maskit (Forthcoming)
Concrete Stephen Parnell (Forthcoming)
Fist by nelle mills (Forthcoming)
Fog by Stephen Sparks (Forthcoming)
Grave Allison C. Meier (Forthcoming)
OK by Michelle McSweeney (Forthcoming)
Pregnancy Test by Karen Weingarten (Forthcoming)
Train by A. N. Devers (Forthcoming)
Wine Meg Bernhard (Forthcoming)

doll

MARIA TERESA HART

BLOOMSBURY ACADEMIC
NEW YORK · LONDON · OXFORD · NEW DELHI · SYDNEY

BLOOMSBURY ACADEMIC
Bloomsbury Publishing Inc
1385 Broadway, New York, NY 10018, USA
50 Bedford Square, London, WC1B 3DP, UK
29 Earlsfort Terrace, Dublin 2, Ireland

BLOOMSBURY, BLOOMSBURY ACADEMIC and the Diana logo are
trademarks of Bloomsbury Publishing Plc

First published in the United States of America 2022

Library of Congress Cataloging-in-Publication Data
Names: Hart, Maria Teresa, author.
Title: Doll / Maria Teresa Hart.
Description: New York: Bloomsbury Academic, 2022. | Series: Object lessons |
Includes bibliographical references and index. | Summary: "An examination
of dolls and how they model an idealized feminine self, instructing girls
what to strive for, and reinforcing dominant patriarchal, heteronormative,
white norms"– Provided by publisher.
Identifiers: LCCN 2022015452 (print) | LCCN 2022015453 (ebook) |
ISBN 9781501380860 (paperback) | ISBN 9781501380877 (epub) |
ISBN 9781501380884 (pdf) | ISBN 9781501380891
Subjects: LCSH: Dolls–History. | Dolls–Social aspects. | Women–Social
conditions. | Sex role. | Gender identity–Social aspects. | Patriarchy–
Psychological aspects.
Classification: LCC GN455.D64 H37 2022 (print) | LCC GN455.D64 (ebook) |
DDC 688.7/221–dc23/eng/20220525
LC record available at https://lccn.loc.gov/2022015452
LC ebook record available at https://lccn.loc.gov/2022015453

ISBN: PB: 978-1-5013-8086-0
ePDF: 978-1-5013-8088-4
eBook: 978-1-5013-8087-7

Series: Object Lessons

Typeset by Deanta Global Publishing Services, Chennai, India
Printed and bound in the United States of America

To find out more about our authors and books visit www.bloomsbury.com
and sign up for our newsletters.

For my mother, who could never deny me a doll.
And for David and Nina.

CONTENTS

INTRODUCTION

In the beginning, there was a doll. Maybe it was a soft bedtime companion or a hard, plastic poseable figure in the latest fashions. Chances are, if you think back to your first watery memories, you'll find a doll scattered among them.

I had a doll then. I must have been two or three. Now I struggle to remember her. Did she come with a name like Raggedy Ann, Samantha, Barbie—or did I invent my own?

Did I beg for her after seeing her in a commercial? Did I point her out to my parents in a toy store as if I was spotting a celebrity? "*There she is! That's her!*"

What games did we play? Mothering? Dress up? Did I bring her on playdates and sleepovers, or did I turn to her for company when I was alone? What was her fate? Did I outgrow her? Did I cut her hair and break her? Shove her in a closet or attic or throw her away?

Or is she with me still, reinforcing my boundaries of womanhood even today?

That dimly remembered first doll was followed by so many others. My toy box was a turbulent kingdom, and I ruled it like a fickle queen, so my favorites changed over the years from Madame Alexander to rag dolls, from Barbies to Cabbage Patch. When American Girl Doll launched, I studied their catalogs like they were a personality quiz: Was I a Kirsten, a Samantha, or a Molly?

At eight years old, midway through my childhood, my family moved to the suburbs of Virginia. The DC Mall became my playground and the Smithsonian museums my personal treasure chest. Their mammoth exhibitions teemed with oddities: trilobite fossils, First Ladies' gowns, taxidermied animals. And, yes, dolls.

Then, one year for Christmas, I received a reproduction porcelain doll purchased from the gift shop of the Smithsonian's National Museum of American History. This was the turning point, after which I became obsessed with dolls, not just as playthings, but also as artifacts and symbols of girlhood. Not my literal girlhood, which would be over in a matter of years, but an idealized, mythical state of young femininity.

I began longing for the real deal—the spot-lit antiques behind the Plexiglas—and I would stay up late into the night, flashlight in hand, studying the Blue Book with its classifications of dolls and their values, losing myself in their history. These dolls didn't have names like Annie or Jo; they had sophisticated, adult-sounding names like Kestner, Jumeau, Ernst Heubach—doll-maker's manufacturing names, which was how antique collectors classified them.

I was still a kid with an allowance that came from doing household chores. I understood there was no number of dishwashers I could unload that would put a Smithsonian-level antique in my eager hands—but I stalked estate sales and scanned classified ads in search of inexpensive castoffs. Maybe I could find a fixer-upper to restore.

Then I discovered doll conventions, the hotel ballrooms or event spaces where vendors and doll-obsessives would gather together in a milling marketplace. I can picture myself then: a gawky tween with a red cross-strap purse holding $80 in cash, a small fortune that represented weeks and weeks of savings. I was an oddity there, the youngest person in attendance by decades. All around me, dolls were set out on skirted tables like prize-winning cakes at a bake-off. The vendors acted as custodians for these treasured possessions, but they were also ambassadors of a kind of lacquered femininity. When I was interested in a doll, the vendor would run through their stats: their age, origin, beauty, popularity, imperfections, etc. Even in my youth, I recognized that these were the same types of assessments that women themselves frequently endured. Did dolls reflect that reality? Or did they somehow establish those expectations?

Some Latin American countries have the tradition of La Ultima Muñeca—The Last Doll—signifying that a girl is all grown up and ready to become a woman. By that measure, I have never reached adulthood. Long after it was appropriate or normal, I continued collecting these miniature beings with their darling expressions and ruffled clothing. A few stowaways followed me to college and then to my first apartment. Even as I write this, there are some a few feet away from me, tucked into shoeboxes and storage containers under the bed and in closets.

But somewhere along the way, I shifted from being a collector to being a questioner, a reporter and examiner of doll culture. As a person drawn to girlie things, I loved dolls the way I adored things like dresses, high heels, makeup—representations of a flouncy, embroidered, ladylike world. But like all these items of formative femininity, I understood that I was highly encouraged by societal norms to embrace them. I was rewarded when I indulged in them, and was ostracized when I didn't. Once I became a questioner, I wanted to interrogate these feelings precisely because they seemed to be reinforced at every turn.

As I grew up, I also became aware that I had internalized so many messages about what it means to be a woman that seemed to have no origin. Did these messages come from teen magazines? By the time I was reading those, it felt like *YM* and *Seventeen* were only confirming my established beliefs. Did they come from my peers? Some, yes. But their ideas of womanhood also had an entry point. I tried to chase these thoughts back to their beginning, and it was like opening a series of nesting dolls, trying to get all the way down to the jelly bean-sized matryoshka that hid at the center. When had I decided how a woman should behave? What she should look like? What she should value? And what was it that convinced me so thoroughly? I thought back to my toy chest and my beloved dolls.

Girls' dolls occupy the opposite space of boys' action figures, which represent masculinity, authority, warfare, and conflict. Ultimately, dolls instruct girls what to strive for in society, often reinforcing dominant patriarchal, heteronormative, white, ableist views around class, race, bodies, history, and celebrity in insidious ways.

While I personally feel drawn to dolls, even to this day, many people experience the opposite sensation, especially when it comes to older models. Picture those unblinking glass eyes. Do you feel a deep chill, an uneasiness, or even a threat of violence? The haunted doll has long been a trope in horror movies, but like many fears, there is some truth at its heart. Dolls are possessed—by our aspirations. They're commonly seen as a tool to teach mothering to young girls, but more often they are avatars of the idealized feminine self.

Think of the way the word "doll" acts as shorthand for a desirable woman. The ragtime song "Oh, You Beautiful Doll," recorded in 1911, is one example of dollhood summing up all a sweetheart's loveliest attributes. "You great big beautiful doll / If you ever leave me how my heart will ache / I want to hug you, but I fear you'd break," goes the chorus.[1]

This association with the word "doll" representing the ideal, lovable woman runs across cultures. When I first moved to New York City as a young Latina, I was nicknamed muñeca (doll) by a Spanish-speaking superintendent. Other languages have this connection, too—ma poupette in French, bambola in Italian. Even in Yiddish, the term of endearment bubbeleh means "little doll" in some translations.

Cosmetic companies use this powerful association to market themselves. Consider Guerlain's K-Doll lipstick,

Lancome's Hypnose Doll Lashes mascara, Anastasia Beverly Hills' American Doll liquid lipstick, Dolly Wink false lashes, Doll Beauty cosmetics, and Doll Face skincare, to name just a few. And then there are all the added cosmetic enhancements, from selfie filters to plastic surgery, that help women achieve that big-eyed, button-nosed, full-lashed, pouty-lips look. These "plastic" procedures intend to inch a person away from flesh and closer to injection-mold perfection.

Yet just as with makeup, dolls aren't the sole domain of girls and women. Flamboyant '80s fitness icon Richard Simmons was such a devoted collector, he appeared on the cover of *Doll Reader* magazine. "This is a man who knows his collection and shows it," the magazine raved in a six-page feature.[2] And famed drag queen Trixie Mattel did a series of YouTube videos parading an ongoing runway of fashion dolls in front of the camera, educating the audience on the finer points of Poodle Parade Barbie. As a child, Trixie was hypnotized by the ads for Movin' Groovin' Barbie and plotted all the ways that a boy could safely obtain this neon '90s muse.[3] For many boys and non-binary kids, owning dolls is a way for them to claim their feminine side and literally play with it. Children of all genders are also drawn to the caregiving side of doll play. This is beautifully captured in the 1972 song "William's Doll," from the *Free to Be You and Me* album. "He wanted a doll to hug and to hold . . . to wash and clean and dress and feed," sing Alan Alda and Marlo Thomas.[4]

But the fact remains that historically dolls have been marketed and directed at young girls, their primary consumers. Whatever messages they contain, positive or negative, are aimed at the pink beating heart of girlhood. And for girls not assigned female at birth, it can be a defining moment when they recognize and confirm their gender through playtime. As trans activist Jazz Jennings told the *New York Times*: "Ever since I was little, I always loved playing with dolls. It was a great way to show my parents that I was a girl, because I could just express myself as I am."[5] At 16, Jennings fulfilled the dream of many little girls, launching a doll version of herself at the Manhattan Toy Fair.

Jennings's generation, who came along decades after mine, still dealt with a sharply divided children's market of pink and blue. Gender, as it's represented in the toy store, is rarely anything beyond binary opposites. Take Barbie as an example: For all her nationalities, professions, races, Barbie rarely acknowledges a version of womanhood that isn't outstandingly feminine. There is no butch Barbie (though I suppose an argument could be made for the commemorative Rosie O'Donnell version). Even when she works construction, Barbie's legs are long and hairless; her lashes are curled; her lips are soft pink; her blonde hair floats past her shoulders.

However, in recent years, as cisgender norms are questioned and non-binary voices are elevated, this division has had a larger reckoning. Those loud and declarative "gender reveal parties," the pink/blue onesies and baby clothes, and other early manifestations of boy/girl compartmentalization are meeting resistance. Progressive parents and caregivers interested in exploring and unpacking the subtle and overt messages given to children through toys are lobbying for better options.

Like all companies, toy companies are in the business of turning a profit—they seek to stay relevant and respond to consumer demand. And as the demand for less gender-polarized dolls grew, Mattel responded in late 2019 with the Creatable World series. "The doll can be a boy, a girl, neither or both," *Time* reported.[6] "Carefully manicured features betray no obvious gender: The lips are not too full, the eyelashes not too long and fluttery, the jaw not too wide. There are no Barbie-like breasts or broad, Ken-like shoulders." But whether this offers an escape from boy-girl classifications or simply a new way to enforce different norms remains to be seen.

Writing for *Slate*, Alex Myers expressed skepticism. "The dolls, in a strange way, present a new sort of paradigm. Their gender expression . . . well, that's limited to three options: feminine and masculine and half-and-half. That's still an incredibly binary way to look at gender. To suggest that the 'other' option to masculine or feminine is 'both' or 'in between' is a basic misunderstanding of how many gender-nonconforming people express their gender."[7]

Nonetheless, this does represent a major shift in the marketplace. "You can sort of chronicle equality in all different forms through the way [Barbie] is produced," Trixie Mattel tells the camera as she shows off her first-edition Black

Barbie with the box's tagline, "She's Black, she's beautiful, she's dynamite!"[8] It's true that because toys reflect society, they will also show the progress mainstream society makes toward equality. However, because toy companies are often responding to cultural moments rather than creating them, they typically come late to the party. For example, Black Barbie didn't come on the market until 1980, six years after Vogue had already published their first cover with Black model Beverly Johnson, and two decades after the Civil Rights Movement won significant legal and social battles against segregation in the United States. (Colored Francie, a Black sidekick character in the line, was introduced in 1967, but she was not the titular Barbie.)

Given that past, are toy companies simply doing public relations damage control with a gender-fluid doll? It does seem convenient that just as outrage around gender policing begins, Mattel launches a product to hopscotch over to the right side of history. But I can measure the amount of time Creatable World has been on the market in months, whereas the influence of dolls and their effect on women goes back centuries. It's that latter timeline that concerns me.

So does that mean that dolls are merely agents of oppression as some feminists have argued? This is reductive thinking. There is still plenty of room for a gray zone, even inside the pastel hues of Barbie's Dream House. As the saying goes, two things can be true at once—or in the case of dolls, two thousand.

Far too often the conversations around dolls are simplified as a celebration or a takedown of the hyper-feminine pink toy aisle. Let's take a new path. Let's look at dolls through a feminist lens, but understand them as complicated objects that can simultaneously expand and contract the realm of possibility for girls. I reject the idea that dolls are simply playthings—instead, I see them as vehicles through which messages about class, race, beauty, history, fame, and selfhood are transferred and internalized.

The chapters that follow are an examination of the toy that defines girlhood—its subconscious instructions, its aspirational traits, and its imposed limitations on the limitless space of make-believe.

PLAY DATE #1

You are holding a book in your hands. But are you also holding a doll? After all, my manuscript is paper, and that's all I need to create a doll.

On any sheet, you could draw a figure—voila! Your paper doll comes to life! I asked illustrator Jenny Odio to draw one for us.

Most paper dolls start in their underwear, a near-nude state. Think of those antiquated comic book ads for X-ray specs, where the wearer sees right through a woman's clothes to the lingerie underneath. Our dolls are always in a state of undress in our hands, inviting games of desire that come when clothing is removed at will.

not a v feminist outlook

1 BODIES THAT MATTER

THE BARBIE DOLL

First, an easy truth: Barbie's body is bonkers.

Thanks to her estimated 18-inch waist and 17 percent body fat, she remains the poster girl for unrealistic and harmful beauty standards foisted on women. Her bullet breasts, handspan hips, thighs like two chopsticks—she's like Mae West pushed through the Play-Doh Fun Factory.

This has been documented at length. Pearl-clutching over Barbie's unrealistic figure is a bit of a media mainstay that's repeated with regularity. A few examples from the last couple of years: In 2009, *Forbes* ran images of a "normal" woman's body next to one photoshopped to Barbie's proportions, elongated and carved out in unnatural ways.[1] In 2013, *Hyperallergic* featured artist Nickolay Lamm's "normal girl" Barbie, which he made with a 3D printer, putting her shorter, broader, but still-slim shape next to the standard-issue doll to drive home the comparison.[2] And in 2019, *Business Insider* published a video taking the measurements for classic Barbie and grafted them onto a woman's likeness, showing a gaunt result.[3] All of these articles arrive at the same conclusion: Barbie is unnatural and sets a dangerous standard of beauty for the young girls that idolize her.

It's for these reasons that Barbie was a target of second-wave feminists to the degree that the National Organization for Women (NOW) organized a protest at the New York Toy Fair with leaflets charging that Barbie "perpetuated sexual stereotypes by encouraging little girls to see themselves solely as mannequins."[4]

I had this stance in my teenage years. At the time, I'd discovered the Riot Grrrl movement, an underground scene fueled by third-wave feminist zines and bands like Bikini Kill and Bratmobile. My uniform for punk shows was frayed baby-doll dresses with combat boots and a studded leather dog collar—a sartorial middle finger to docile femininity. In this new environment, Barbie became the enemy for all the usual reasons. I felt this acutely as a Latina that lacked the doll's coloring and long willowy limbs.

I had plenty of company in this regard. The excellent young adult book *The Good, the Bad, and the Barbie* collects testimonials from women and girls speaking to their relationship with the iconic toy, and plenty of these show a link between the doll and low self-esteem: "Barbie has this perfect body and now every girl is trying to have her body because they are so unhappy with themselves," one says.[5]

In high school, I wrote my own version of this criticism in the zine I published with my best friend. My approach was a laughably bad poem about how Barbie made me feel less-than. Against a black-and-white photo of model Kirsty Hume, my doll stand-in, I typed:

Oh Barbie, Barbie burning bright
I heard your legs rubbing together in the back of the closet
Like an insect
But did you hear
My anguished screams?

I'll spare you the rest. Obviously, Courtney Love did it better when she wrote the now-famed '90s Hole song "Doll Parts," which came out during peak third-wave years. In it, Love sings, "I am doll eyes, doll mouth, doll legs," but despite being this pretty object, she's still subjected to being broken, devalued ("dog bait"), and hurt. The song ends with Love shouting over and over "Someday, you will ache like I ache."[6] The cover of the single had a Barbie bridal playset, including a tiny lace dress, white pumps, a veil, a little dove, and a blue garter no bigger than a TicTac.

Love has stated that "Doll Parts" was about the romantic rejection she felt early in her courtship with Kurt Cobain. But it's easy to interpret these lyrics in a more universal way as being about the lookism women feel on a daily basis—the pressure to be doll-like in appearance, knowing that society will still find you both "fake" and disposable, ending in anguish.

Whatever politics are at play in the song, Love undercuts them with one key detail: She herself adheres to Barbie's aesthetic. In the music video of "Doll Parts," the camera lingers on her slim body, long limbs, pale white skin, bleach-blond hair, cherry-red lips, and ruffled minidress; she is actively upholding doll-like beauty standards while challenging them through her lyrics and loud, distortion-heavy music.[7] In more recent years, the Hole front-woman admitted to cosmetic surgery and gave dieting tips during interviews.[8, 9]

Being conventionally attractive allows Love the privilege of being heard. The message here is "I am entitled to a public voice because I am attractive and that gives me worth." In other words, only women that uphold the Barbie standard can critique it. In order to be heard, you have to be operating from inside the system.

It's this double standard that feels like the bruise on Barbie's shining apple of achievement. Supporters of Barbie will point to the fact that she represents limitless possibility; she's an illustration for all the things little girls can become, breaking the glass ceiling and reaching beyond our current reality. (Think: President Barbie.) As one fan put it in Stone's book, "I loved dressing her in business suits and she often wore a hat and carried a briefcase. Today, I am a decorator, and I swear those early experiences of putting clothes together helped lead me to this career."[10]

Barbie also suggests that the perfect heterosexual romantic partner, one that matches your interests, is waiting for you. Whether you love line-dancing, cooking, or "earring magic"—whatever that is—there is a corresponding Ken at the ready. In Barbie's world, Barbie rules, while Ken conforms to her, the dutiful eye-candy prince on her arm. This stands in contrast to a century of women's media that insists you should take up your partner's hobbies and interests, centering his experiences, to have a successful relationship. ("When you're hanging out with guy friends, pay attention to what they talk about and what cracks them up," advises *Seventeen's Ultimate Guide to Guys*. "Being totally comfortable in guy-world helps you hold your own around a cutie you like."[11])

There's a subtext to all this promised freedom of choice: Women must pass through the keyhole of Barbie's exaggerated hourglass proportions in order to reach this Nirvana. Who else is allowed to pick from an endless lineup of professions and romantic partners but a young, slim, white, blond, able-bodied, model-beautiful woman?

This promise land—limitless career potential, romantic interests galore—is part of the reason several women have seen Barbie as a blueprint worth duplicating on their own bodies, despite her drastic proportions. Throughout the last 60-plus years, many women have pursued this goal via cosmetic surgery, slavish diets, spray tans, and makeup. From Rachel Evans in the U.K. to Nannette Hammon in the U.S., these women are dubbed "The Human Barbie" by the media.[12,13] Their devotion—physically, financially—to plastic surgery brings to mind Aqua's 1997 ironic pop song "Barbie Girl," ("Life in plastic! It's fantastic!"[14])

One of the latest Barbie doppelgangers to claim the title is Valeria Lukyanova, whose uncanny looks were a feature story in *GQ*. "In the flesh—the little of it that she hasn't whittled away with what she says is exercise and diet—Valeria looks almost exactly like Barbie," Michael Idov writes. "Her beauty, though I hesitate to use the term, is pitched at the exact precipice where the male gaze curdles in on itself. Her features are the features we men playfully ascribe to ideal women . . . Except we don't expect them to comply with this oppressive fantasy so fully."[15]

And Barbie doesn't just model bodily perfection; she also models body dissatisfaction. One infamous doll, Sleepover Barbie, came with a tiny scale, as if the primary group activity for young women is policing their weight. Even more damning was her other accessory—a miniature book called *How to Lose Weight*. Its only advice? "Don't eat." (This book made another appearance with Babysitting Barbie.)

Conclusion: Barbie equals a negative symbol of the patriarchy. But then there is another truth, one that came before my teen rage. In order to recall it, I have to go back to the early days, both for myself and for Barbie.

*   *   *

I first met Barbie during my Saturday-morning-cartoon lineup. Sandwiched between episodes of *Muppet Babies* and

Snorks was her salute to girlhood. Her commercial had a hooky jingle with the lyrics, "We girls can do anything!"[16] Judging by all her various careers—Astronaut! Surgeon! Chef! Canadian Mountie!—that anthem seems apt. But now that I know Barbie's past, this laundry list of occupations feels like a smokescreen for her original profession, perhaps the world's oldest.

Barbie began life not as a doll but as a cartoon called Bild-Lilli, a character in the pages of the German tabloid *Bild-Zeitung* in 1952. These were Germany's lean post-war years, and Lilli was a scrappy escort using her figure and her fast wit to get by. She was often depicted in her swimsuit or underwear, which she flaunted with a few choice one-liners. In one famed panel, Lilli is getting charged with indecency for wearing a bikini, and she shoots back at the police officer, "Oh, and in your opinion, which part should I take off?" In another, Lilli is covering up her nudity with a few sheets of newsprint as she explains to a friend, "We had a fight, and he took back all the presents he gave me."

On and off the page, Lilli was a hit with the fellas. German men appreciated her big almond-shaped eyes, Aryan blonde hair, extreme hourglass proportions, and her up-for-anything attitude. In 1955, a Bild-Lilli doll was launched, though it never made it to toy stores. Instead, it was sold in cigar shops and liquor stores to adult fans. In both style and marketing, Bild-Lilli had more in common with inflatable sex dolls than kids' playthings. It was a frequent bachelor gag gift—a pocket-sized vixen men could undress at will.

The toy's box showed a cartoon Lilli exhaling a cigarette, her breasts practically falling out of her slit-to-the-navel white mini dress.

Bild-Lilli's story could have ended here, as a fetish object somewhere between striptease "naked lady pens" and nude women on mudflaps; but like many Hollywood starlets, Lilli was "discovered." While on a trip to Europe, Mattel's founder Ruth Handler spotted Lilli and had a light-bulb moment. Here was a toy that girls could dress up, like a three-dimensional paper doll. This also coincided with a Second World War boom in plastics, meaning that cheap raw materials were at the ready.

In America, the name and market audience changed, but little else did. When Barbie hit toy store shelves in the spring of 1959, her bullet breasts, nipped waist, long legs, blond hair, arched eyebrows, and sly side-eye were all pure Lilli, which is to say saturated with sex appeal. In her swimsuit and sunglasses, she looked like a Betty Grable-type pin-up. As Handler predicted, Barbie's high-heeled feet were jumping into a blank space in the market. At the time, toy shops were a sea of baby dolls for playing mother. Barbie let little girls play something else—the vamp.

Today, Barbie doesn't own up to her origins, leaning heavily on a mantra of girl power through various careers and identities. The current tagline—"You can be anything"—feels like a rehash of my childhood jingle. But now I can see beyond the empowered superwoman persona to the unrepentant coquette she once was. After all, Barbie still needs someone to foot her bills. Her new sugar daddy? The children who buy her heaps of designer clothes, sports cars, and on and on. While the client might have changed, the game is the same—femininity is still for sale.

In my Saturday-morning-cartoon days, I had no knowledge of this backstory. I was only too happy to lavish Barbie with material goods and keep her in the lifestyle she was accustomed to. My birthday lists were full of requests for things like lamé dresses and Dream Houses and pink corvettes and horses with brushable manes. In 1992, Teen Talk Barbie was met with controversy for uttering the phrase "Math class is tough," potentially discouraging young girls from going into STEM fields. But I find her other phrases—"I love to shop!" and "Will we ever have enough clothes?"—far more telling.

Materialism was part of Barbie's advertised appeal; sexual liberation wasn't. Still, under the taffeta gowns and power suits, I could see Lilli there, the ghost in Barbie's shell. Apart from dressing them in various outfits, my number one way of "playing Barbie" could be best described as a raging sexcapade. Ken was a late addition to my toys, but no matter—my Barbies could have racy affairs with my stuffed animals, and with each other. My mother still laughs at the memory of finding my Barbies in improbable sex positions— balanced on their heads with their legs in an upside-down gymnast's split, another doll straddled on top like a Jenga tower of plastic limbs. I didn't know the mechanics exactly, but I was certain that this was what these dolls were made to do.

I grew up Catholic, and Barbie was my escape, my way of enacting fantasies. This was many years before the phrase "slut-shaming" became common parlance. Dolls, like women themselves, are routinely divided into a Madonna/whore dichotomy. Baby dolls, which encourage maternal role-playing, lie in the former category. Barbie and her Bratz descendants are some of the few toys in the latter camp. As a plaything, Barbie allowed me to safely try on adult sexuality. And though in Barbie's world hetero-normality ruled—with Ken as a constant escort—she still provided girls a tool through which to imagine themselves as sexually empowered women with a partner who valued them, which was exactly what I was exploring in my games.

I wasn't alone in this approach to Barbie either. Stone's book also documents girls that were drawn to this type of play, including one whose favorite game was "Barbie at a nudist colony." As another woman put it, reflecting on her playtime, "How did I . . . play with my Barbies? I took off all her clothes and sent her looking for love. My Barbie got around."[17] Writer Tracie Egan Morrissey also explores this type of play for *Jezebel* in an article titled, "Growing Up, Everyone Did Dirty Things With Their Barbies," which included comments from readers about playing "Playboy Bunny Barbie/Stripper Barbie/Gotta-Get-Paid-For-Sex-to-Pay-The-Rent-Barbie."[18]

However, Lilli didn't just evolve into Barbie. Her road forked. On one side, she became a toy; on the other, a sexual prop. In his book *The Sex Doll: A History*, Anthony Ferguson points to Bild-Lilli as the origin of a new commercial market. While sex dolls had been around for over a century (with masturbatory figures for sailors dubbed "dames de voyage") Lilli is seen by Ferguson as the industrial launching pad for the mass production and global marketplace of these dolls—everything from cheap inflatable dolls to high-end silicon models with vibrating or lubricated interiors.[19]

What happens when Barbie trades hands from young girls to heterosexual men? The element of identification with Barbie drops away—she becomes not the self you are exploring, but the objectified "other" you are manipulating. The result is a calcification of the sexual power dynamics between men and women. For some men, this flips the equation of "idealized woman equals doll" in the other direction: Sex dolls now equal the idealized woman. Or as one fanatic of the high-end brand Sidore told *The Atlantic*: "There was never a moment when [Sidore]—or any doll, for that matter—was merely an object to me." He describes his premium model as his wife.[20]

But if these dolls are seen as beings, they raise the question: What being would submit themselves to a lifetime of mute, passive, sexual use with no consideration for their own needs? Who could endure that without an ocean of rage under that placid surface? It's this fear, a fear of retribution by animated dolls, that was captured in the science-fiction film *Ex Machina*.[21] In it, a programmer, Caleb, arrives at a remote residence to meet a female robot, Ava, for what he believes is a Turing Test—to determine just how much she can "pass" as a human. Ava, who lives a cloistered life under the surveillance of her creator, tries to appeal to Caleb by wearing a wig and a soft feminine sweater over her android exterior. There are also hints of abuse, potentially sexual, between Ava and her creator. Ultimately, she wins Caleb over; he releases her from her enclosure, only to have her turn on him in violence.

The idea of Ava may sound like pure Hollywood nonsense, but in truth, we are getting closer and closer to a robot doll that can echo our humanity. Consider BINA48, modeled after the real human being Bina Aspen, a Black woman who was married to Martine Rothblatt, a prominent CEO in the biotech industry. BINA48 was created using Aspen's memories. She can perform 64 facial gestures and has facial recognition software to identify repeat visitors. Tellingly, BINA48 doesn't have a body—she is a bust, just a head and shoulders set on a tabletop.

In a feature for *The Believer*, Amy Kurzweil meets BINA and Bruce Duncan, her handler. At one point, Duncan tells Kurzweil about his disappointment that at a Q&A demonstration for BINA48 one man shouted out, "What's your bra size?" To Kurzweil, this question doesn't shock her. "Female robots do risk perpetuating this fantasy for some, of 'women devoid of humanity,'" she replies. Duncan agrees noting, "With AI, we're creating a high-resolution mirror, and the higher-resolution it gets, the more we see who we really are, and that's troubling." Later, they discuss the complications of adding a body to BINA. Kurzweil wonders: "You're going to see people interacting with BINA48 in ways that perpetuate racism and misogyny. How much more complicated does it get if you give her a body?"[22]

That race is a factor for BINA48 means that the high-resolution mirror she provides also shines a powerful reflection on the racism people bring to their interactions with others. Duncan remembers one visit in particular where four women said to him, "Why did you make her an angry Black woman?"

This points to the fact that when our bodies are read by others, they aren't only registering attractiveness or sexual allure. Physically, we are also a collection of variables that are used as racial indicators. In *The Atlantic*, Ta-Nehisi Coates writes that "no coherent, fixed definition of race actually exists . . . Our notion of what constitutes 'white' and what constitutes 'Black' is a product of social construct."[23] At different points in history and at different points on the globe, that definition has changed, usually to suit the wealthy ruling class. Nevertheless, human beings continue to ascribe categories of race to skin pigment, eye color, hair texture, width or length of facial features, etc.—and this feels even more pronounced when it comes to toys, as those physical aspects are a doll's entirety.

The prototype for Barbie came from Germany with little modification, so naturally, it reflects Eurocentric, Aryan beauty standards. Non-white Barbie dolls were introduced almost a decade later, starting in 1967 with Colored Francie. (Black dolls Francie, Christie, Cara, and Julia would remain Skipper-esque sidekicks until 1980 when the first Black

Barbie was released.) Mattel used an established mold for Francie, only changing the color of the plastic. We still see the same button nose, narrow hips, and flowing hair used on her white counterpart. Essentially, the company was coloring inside the same lines, just swapping out the crayon. The subtext here is almost too obvious—women of color must press themselves into the mold of white women's features in order to attain the same level of visibility and success.

Asian depictions of Barbie have been similarly flawed. It wasn't until 1981 that Mattel released its first Asian Barbie, named Oriental Barbie. This doll did have a new face mold, a good step toward accurate representation. But, as Kelly Kasulis wrote for the *Boston Globe*, "Oriental Barbie was a catchall of Asian cultures," complete with a fan and a red-and-gold dress illustrating "a lingering Orientalism."[24]

Other Asian dolls would follow: Korean, Japanese, Malaysian Barbies, and more, part of a new Dolls of the World collection. While these models did expand on representation, a lingering question remains: Who is their intended audience? All of these dolls are dressed in traditional garb (e.g., the Japanese one in a kimono, the Korean one in a hanbok), emphasizing their foreign exoticism rather than depicting them as typical teens of the 1980s. The packaging on these dolls also explained each dolls' home country. "Korea is a rabbit-shaped country divided into two parts: North Korea and South Korea" read Korean Barbie's box—facts that would fall into the "no duh" category for any Korean-American girl. It seems rather than envisioning these dolls for an Asian consumer to see themselves, they offered a "cultural safari," as Kasulis puts it, to white consumers, tapping into a larger globalism trend that was taking place in the '80s, from "We Are the World" sing-alongs to United Colors of Benetton ads.

Despite these issues, I was impressed when Chilean Barbie was released in 1998, reflecting my own Latina roots. Someone at Mattel really knows their stuff, I remember thinking as I studied her traditional huaso costume and her white kerchief, ready for dancing cueca. She was blanquita (pale) for a Latina, but then so am I. Chilean culture is still largely unknown in the U.S., lumped into a "South of the Border" persona—at times I'd have to explain to my classmates that piñatas and burritos weren't a part of my upbringing. Yet the designers at Barbie headquarters nailed it. I wasn't her only admirer; my mother bought this doll and displayed it in her home office despite being 50 years older than the target demographic, seeing something of herself there.

But even as Mattel continues to spin the globe and expand Barbie's nationalities—Nigerian! Polynesian! Puerto Rican!—there is no doubt that the default "standard" Barbie is blonde, white, and Germanic. All other Barbies must be qualified with an added adjective: Black, Asian, Mexican, etc. This brings to mind Toni Morrison's famed quote in response to the term African American: "In this country, American means white; everyone else has to hyphenate."

These global Barbies also tumble into a void once they're unboxed. Unlike white Barbie, they don't have a full world built around them. You can buy Malaysian Barbie, but there's no Malaysian Ken to pair her with. And once she's shed her batik costume, there are no subsequent Malaysian outfits for her closet. Like so many immigrants, she's forced to assimilate into a white world, to move into white Barbie's house, to wear her clothes, to date her Ken.

White Barbie remains the default Barbie because she has never budged from getting top billing. As Koa Beck writes in *White Feminism*, "Ceding power not only means welcoming brown and Black people to your meetings—it inherently asks you to give up something too."[25] Or put in Barbie terms, it isn't enough to add "diverse" bandmates to the Barbie and the Rockers band. A truly anti-racist toy would have white Barbie stepping aside as the front-woman to let Black Barbie take her place on lead vocals.

Upending Barbie's white, Eurocentric dominance isn't easy. Just consider Nicki Minaj. The rapper has built up an entire lexicon of Barbie references for herself. Her physical aesthetic—hyper-curvaceous silhouettes, candy-colored accessories, giant fluttering doll eyes—play into her alter ego Harajuku Barbie. That moniker has popped up in her songs ("Barbie Dreams," "Barbie Tingz"), in her signoff ("It's Barbie, bitch"), and even in her fan base ("Barbies" or "Barbz"). In 2011, Mattel cemented the association by creating a one-of-a-kind Minaj Barbie doll for a charitable auction. "I definitely don't think that when we say 'Barbie,' we're thinking of the plastic little dolls with blond hair anymore," Minaj told MTV. "It's really how we've come to define ourselves."[26]

But for all Minaj's efforts to uncouple the name "Barbie" from the image of a white, blonde doll and replace it with her own self-image, one only needs to do a Google image search on the name to see the reality: row after row of pale faces and frozen smiles. It's a hall of mirrors with the same white icon repeated to infinity. Minaj—in the flesh or in doll form—is nowhere to be seen.

It's precisely this racial blind spot that left Barbie vulnerable to competition. Her challenger? Mattel's prodigal daughter—Bratz.

As Orly Lobel documents in her book, *You Don't Own Me*, Bratz began as the brainchild of Carter Bryant, a Mattel employee who was burned out toiling away on projects like Goddess of Beauty Barbie, an Aphrodite-themed doll. On company leave in 1998, he spotted a group of teens full of fresh, youthful energy, and sketched out a design—the anti-Barbie. Her body was distorted, with a miniaturized figure and a lollipop head. Her face, likewise, was exaggerated, all lips and cat eyes. And her clothes were full-blown streetwear—baggy jeans, midriff-baring tops, beanies. Bryant saw Bratz as a quartette of multiracial dolls: Black, white, Asian, and Latina. But he didn't center the white doll or give her the marquee name, as in Barbie's universe. She was simply part of a set of friends.[27]

Later, when Bryant took his idea to rival toy company MGA, it was the CEO's daughter, 12-year-old Jasmin Larian, who cast the deciding vote on a mockup. "There was nothing diverse on the market at that time. It was just this blonde, blue-eyed girl," she told *Vice* 18 years later, now an adult and MGA employee. "I was like 'These are so cool! I need these!'" Bratz also sported the clothes Larian and her friends were actually wearing. "Barbie is more Rodeo Drive. We're more streetwear Melrose: mix and match, make your own clothes."[28]

Originally, Bryant pitched Bratz as racially delineated. But MGA's CEO, Isaac Larian, steered away from this approach and advocated to keep them "ethnically ambiguous," informed by his own perspective as an Iranian Jew. Instead of applying checkboxes to each racial type, Bratz allowed girls to self-identify with whichever doll spoke to them.

The dolls were a sensation, destroying Barbie's lock on the toy market. The two companies, Mattel and MGA, would duke it out in round after round of legal fights over who truly owned Bryant's creation. But outside the courtroom, Bratz would face their own cultural battle. The American Psychological Association called out the dolls for their "sexualization of young girls."[29] Online parenting forums put the dolls on blast, and then there was the *Saturday Night Live* segment honoring Barbie's 50th anniversary. In it, Kristin Wiig, dressed as a first-edition Barbie doll, describes her birthday party: "My friends had a party for me—Midge, Skipper, Black Barbie . . . " Here the audience laughs. "Well that sounds fun," host Seth Meyers replies. "It was," Wiig/ Barbie confirms, "until a slutty Bratz doll showed up and cut somebody."[30]

Does the audience understand the hypocrisy of one scantily clad doll calling another doll "slutty"? And then there is Wiig's punchline, which doesn't just accuse Bratz for being overly sexual, but also as angry and violent—another reflection of BINA48 supposed angry Black woman.

This insult, "slut," surfaces again and again as a put-down for these dolls. When *Vice* askes a Bratz designer what the biggest misconception is about these toys, he readily answers, "That they're sluts." But he dismisses this. "I feel like no matter how you dress, it doesn't mean that someone knows who you are inside." Jasmin Larian also rejects the criticism that they're "so-called sluts." She says, "As a kid, I thought they were really cute and cool and just wanted to hang out with them."[31]

Looking at the doll's physique now, I see nothing more pronounced or sexual than the average fashion doll. The Bratz body is almost an afterthought, overshadowed by her bobblehead. Her proportions are less extreme than Barbie's, her bust smaller, her waist-to-hip ratio less severe. Could it be all this talk about Bratz as "sluts" is simply a racist reaction to the depiction of a young woman of color in urban streetwear? This would track with the Georgetown University study "Girlhood Interrupted: The Erasure of Black Girl's Childhood," which demonstrated that adults perceive Black girls as "much less innocent" than white girls. "Black girls . . . are adultified, sexualized, and deemed overly aggressive from a young age," writer Jonita Davis paraphrased in the *Washington Post*.[32]

The Barbie/Bratz racial divide was even more pronounced during the civil unrest following George Floyd's murder. MGA made a statement early on, posting on May 30th to the Bratz Instagram account: "Our hearts break for George Floyd and the Black community. Bratz has always been and will always be about diversity and inclusivity. It is all our responsibility to take a stand against racism, and we can't call ourselves inclusive while staying silent about these social injustices right in front of us."[33]

The outpouring of love on social media was immediate. "Bratz was the first toy brand I remember that really popularized Black/minority ethnic dolls," one fan wrote. "They've been amazing for years!" Another used this moment to throw down the gauntlet to Mattel: "We stan Bratz. Barbie has 24 hours to respond. #BlackLivesMatter."[34]

As it happens, Barbie would take more than 24 hours to reply. Her statement came later, on June 12th, committing to a series of actions including "Elevating Black voices on our team" and "Working with retail to ensure diversity is represented." While this is a positive and proactive reply, it feels like the post from a white friend promising to "do better."[35] As a follow-up in October, Mattel released an animated vlog with (white) Barbie and her friend Nikki (perhaps a nod to Minaj) discussing everyday racism. Nikki, who is Black, describes moments like being stopped by security for looking suspicious, much to Barbie's shock.[36] It's a thoughtful, educational conversation for kids to hear, but two questions come to mind: Why isn't Black Barbie the narrator? And why do Nikki's experiences have to be framed by white Barbie's reactions?

Barbie and Mattel's entry into a conversation about racism points to the pitfalls of representation as the only goal. It's not enough to put the image of a beautiful woman of color into the world without any values to back it up. As Toni Morrison said about the phrase "Black Is Beautiful": "The implication was that once we had convinced everybody, including ourselves, of our beauty, then, then . . . what? Things would change? We could assert ourselves? Make demands? White people presumably had no objection to beautiful people."[37] It seems obvious that beauty alone is a very poor shield against racial violence and prejudice.

Did this have any impact on Barbie? In a word, no. As 2020 rolled on, various celebrities were canceled on social media after controversies linked to racism and sexism. But in this sea of scrutiny, Barbie's plastic body just keeps bobbing along. By the end of 2020, Barbie hit record sales of $1.35 billion, putting that same curvaceous figure into the hands of the next generation.[38]

*　*　*

When I take Barbie's body into my own hands, I don't see a molded figure so much as a prism. We beam into this object an ideal of womanhood, and what gets refracted out is a spectrum of beauty standards, sexual fantasies, consumer excess, and racial categorization. In that way, Barbie does inhabit the same space as the modern everywoman, just not as her manufacturers would have you believe. It isn't because she's a successful career woman or a liberated girl-about-town. It's simply because she is representing a woman in a woman's body, and like me, she is subjected to all the restrictions and judgment that go along with it.

PLAY DATE #2

Now surely our paper doll can't be left to shiver in the nude! She needs clothes. Lots and lots of clothes! You can't assess a person's place in society when they're naked. Clothing gives context. Through dress, we can categorize others: This woman is an executive. This one is a model. This one is a nurse. This one is a punk rocker. We can also place them on a timeline: Here's a Victorian queen, a 1700s peddler, a medieval milkmaid.

We can start with a single outfit. Dress up is part of the fun, so let's make this one really flamboyant. Why hold back on ruffles? On lace? On a wildly ostentatious dress? After all, this is just paper, so it's all pretend. We can add them all in. Jewelry, too! A bib of paper diamonds for our paper lady. Now we have a dress for our Victorian doll.

In play, we can be anyone we want! Why would we choose to be anything other than extremely rich?

2 ALL THAT MONEY CAN BUY

THE PORCELAIN DOLL

- Victorian flaws

- acted as an instruction manuel for how people should act

Some kids love trains, or LEGO, or Pokémon cards. My childhood obsession was porcelain dolls—the legit, real deal, came-from-some-dead-grandma's-attic kind. As you can imagine, this wasn't an interest shared with my classmates, who preferred Barbie. But I was always drawn to the Victorians' overblown ornamentation: their lace-collared Gibson girls, beveled perfume bottles, claw-footed toast racks, and gold-leaf teacups. It didn't hurt that I'd also watched Winona Ryder swish through one bustle-backed period drama after another. What kind of people had special silver forks just for ice cream? *My* type of people, I decided.

When I visited my local doll and toy museum in Northern Virginia, the 100-year-old dolls just beyond reach filled me with a wooziness that could only be described as *I want*. And so, I began the hunt through estate sales and country auctions and later eBay to chase down antique dolls of my own. The few I did collect were not my toys so much as my treasures. They served about as much purpose as a claw-footed toast rack, which is to say they were useless. But their function didn't matter to me, just as it hadn't mattered to the Victorians. What mattered was beauty, refinement, and . . . well, I wasn't sure exactly. I couldn't really articulate why these decorative dolls had become such a mania for me.

I loved gazing at them in all their finery, but what I didn't realize at the time was that I'd fallen into the same flawed thinking the Victorians had, idolizing porcelain dolls for all the wrong reasons.

* * *

The Victorian era was a time of Big New Ideas. There were new thoughts about wedding dresses (make 'em white!) seances (for a good time, call the dead), and childhood. The latter, especially, marked a kind of social revolution. In the 17th and early 18th centuries, children were seen as inherently sinful. It was a spare-the-rod-and-spoil-the-child time, where parents had a moral calling to keep their kids from succumbing to their darker, devilish impulses. Or, as Therese Oneill put it in her book *Ungovernable*, "Your child is imbued with what religious leaders call Original Sin. And it's your job as a parent to tidy up the moral mess you gave birth to."[1]

One of those religious leaders was John Wesley, founder of the Methodist Church, who preached that parents must "break [children's] will, that you may save their soul" from what he considered "inherent wickedness." Beyond the pulpit, philosopher John Locke—who wrote his own parenting book, *Some Thoughts on Education*—was less damning. But he still saw childhood as merely functional. The end goal? Produce an adult who would perform their station in life. Play was only useful if it built good habits. And an overly tender mother, God forbid, could derail all of this.[2]

This stance began to soften in the 1800s, as romantic poets like William Wordsworth and William Blake linked childhood with a state of purity and innocence. Pre-Raphaelite artists like John Everett Millais painted children not as stiff miniature adults but as young individuals with a vulnerable sweetness, all apple cheeks and corkscrew curls. And everywhere, as Miriam Forman-Brunell notes in *Made to Play House,* there was the "pervasive image of the angelic Victorian girl."[3]

In this sea change, childhood morphed into a heavily romanticized, dreamy time of purity and innocence, a fragile moment that required protection. Yet it was clear, only upper- and middle-class youth would be sheltered, with working-class children as young as four or five forced to do labor in mines, textile mills, and other rapidly developing industries. When it came to those children, Locke's view still stood: He advocated enlisting the very youngest into labor, arguing that even a three-year-old could be put to work with little more than bread and maybe some warm water-gruel if it happened to be cold outside.[4] Victorian toys, mostly created for wealthy children, embodied this schism. And lavish porcelain bisque dolls, often depicting high society with garments of velvet and lace, could be considered the grandest spectacle of that hypocrisy. Gilded Age dolls expressly "fostered conspicuous consumption, ritual, and display," Forman-Brunell writes.[5]

The dolls themselves were a miniature model of the cycle of fashion consumerism: new outfits, new hairdos, new accessories and furnishings for these bisque beauties. It was all a dress rehearsal for the consumer cycle of womanhood. Forman-Brunell notes, "Some of the most expensive French fashion dolls in the 1870s and 1880s arrived with fully packed trunks [of clothes], often tripling the price of the dolls alone."[6]

These dolls had a fashionista forerunner: mini mannequins. The French royal court would ship these fully decked out in the latest styles so aristocracy in other countries could copy them for their closets. Essentially, they were the 1700s version of flipping through *Vogue*. But once the royal seamstresses were done with these dress dummies, they had a second life. Antonia Fraser writes in *Dolls*, "When they had served their fashion purpose, many of them found their way into nurseries as playthings."[7] A few fashion dolls were created just to delight, too. Marie Antoinette commissioned fashion dolls for her sisters and mother, not necessarily to pattern dresses, but simply as an object to enjoy. It's these three-dimensional fashion plates that set the stage for the elaborate porcelain dolls of the 19th and 20th centuries.

In that respect, porcelain dolls were nothing new. The toy-as-status-symbol connection has long been established. In the Middle Ages, clay toys were the playthings of the people—easily made and widely available, whereas ornate knight dolls with jousting accessories were the rare, exquisite items reserved for the children of royalty.[8] This division goes all the way back to antiquity. Consider the Crepereia Tryphaena, the sarcophagus of a Roman woman from 2 or 3 AD, which contained a beautifully crafted jointed doll made of wood. Death is the great equalizer: All skeletons look the same. But this doll acted as a stand-in for her owner's body. When Tryphaena's physical presence could no longer communicate her status, her doll's sculpted face, molded hair, and fine details were able to deliver the message.

But the boom in doll production was new, thanks to a number of societal factors glomming together in the 1800s. The first was a boost in personal income for the middle class in America, which drove a spending spree on European goods. The aim of acquiring these items was to emulate the upper class who were, in turn, emulating European elites. Real estate for nursery space also expanded for middle-class families, giving more room for dolls and a designated place for playtime. An explosion of shopping venues followed these developments—from ritzy department stores to the encyclopedic mail-order catalogs to mushrooming chain stores—providing ample toy-buying opportunities. That buying went into overdrive on Christmas, which solidified into a national U.S. holiday and a Santa-themed gift-giving bonanza in the 1870s. And finally, busy parents with fewer children came to see dolls as a good surrogate for companionship.[9] All this was coupled with innovations in mass production and the dawn of the factory. The result: Porcelain dolls were poised for a takeover.

In America, these dolls were imported from doll-makers in France and Germany, the latter absolutely dominating the toy market, accounting for two-thirds of all of Europe's doll output. French dolls didn't have the same turnout, but they commanded top dollar then and now. German makers like Armand Marseille were more affordable, but they were still "dolls in the grand manner," as Fraser puts it. And that grand manner was porcelain.

In *The New Yorker*, Thessaly La Force recounts Europe's feverish obsession with porcelain. It had arrived from China in the 14th century, and from the beginning it was considered "white gold." "Porcelain is for the refined, for the ruling class, with all of its power and privilege," La Force writes, describing the way emperors and kings craved it. "This level of materialism, after all, is never about necessity."[10]

There is a racial component to the material, too; as La Force puts it, "the most fraught symbolism of porcelain is its whiteness."[11] The milky absence of color has been compared in flattering ways to pale skin. A "porcelain complexion," unmarked by sun or time, was a beauty standard of the Victorian era, with an armada of accessories—parasols, gloves, powders—to shield white women from obtaining a tan, something associated with laboring outside more than beachside lounging. It was precisely this analogy of porcelain as exemplary skin that made it the ideal surface for doll-makers.

In doll production, porcelain was used on the most visible part, the part put on display to the public: the head. Unlike previous China dolls, porcelain heads were made with an unglazed biscuit firing, bisque for short, giving the substance a more lifelike matte finish that could be painted. Bodies could be made from a variety of materials, kid leather or "composition" (a papier-mâché-type mix of sawdust and glue). The result was far less lifelike, but this bumpy result would be hidden under clothing, so its presentation mattered far less. Even American doll-makers would frequently use European heads on their locally made bodies, essentially disguising their domestic products and adding European accreditation.

The fragility of these kiln-baked faces was part of their appeal: To make something this delicate and place it into the hands of a child was to publicly declare you had the money to fix or replace it. And so, these dolls not only presented an idealized image of the wealthy, but were themselves symbols of being part of the upper class, their very nature communicating the relationship of rich to poor.

Not all porcelain dolls were white. Depictions of other races existed, but they were a rarity and heavily otherized as an exotic addition to a white child's toy chest. Manufacturers typically used the same molds for white dolls and added a tint to the porcelain base and changed the costume to reflect a different nationality (much as Mattel would do with their Colored Francie doll almost a century later). Still, the default porcelain doll, by a huge majority, was one with a pale face and glass eyes. Even that eye color went in a lighter and lighter direction. Before the 1830s, the most popular doll eye color was brown, but the accession of Queen Victoria established a preference for blue-eyed dolls reflecting the queen's own irises—a shift that still has a hold on the marketplace today.[12]

Some of these doll parts were used in fanciful automatons—figurines that could mimic lifelike gestures like walking or waiving a handkerchief. Automata wasn't new on the scene; for centuries, inventors and clockmakers used their skills to create extravagant moving tableaus and figures. Movies like *Hugo* and *Jingle Jangle* fictionalize these whirling inventions, but their reality was almost as fantastical. Imagine dolls that, with the turn of a key, could draw portraits or play the flute. One disturbing version of these automatons depicted Black servants at work, implying that Black labor and servitude were automatic and expected.[13] The Victorian era's versions included Thomas Edison's "talking doll," a porcelain doll with a pint-sized phonograph tucked inside (though this contraption was a malfunctioning flop). These mechanical embellishments were one more lavish feature added to an already luxurious toy, amplifying their message even louder.

As automatons indicate, the Victorians liked a "more is more" approach, and the class signifier of expensive dolls were often layered with other indicators. The ultimate example of this would be the child portrait. In an attempt to display their newly acquired social rank, "many middle-class parents hired itinerant artists to paint portraits of their daughters holding dolls resembling fashionable ladies."[14] This custom would continue throughout the 1800s, as the paintbrush gave way to the photograph. The resulting portrait was hardly nursery decor, but an object for parents to indicate that their status allowed for material excess at every household level. And by some accounts, it's the parents that delighted in these dolls the most. They relished the new leisure activity of toy shopping and the selection of another decorative object for the home.[15] For a child, however, a heavy porcelain doll had all the cuddle-factor of cradling a China vase.

So how *did* little girls play with these toys? The doll play itself was often a rehearsal for a lifetime of class-signaling. In the Victorian era, middle- and upper-class women were enclosed in domestic space, but doll play would frequently focus on those moments of public interaction. Tea parties were a popular play-date event, but so were "receptions" or the act of paying a visit. Some dolls were even equipped with miniature calling cards and visiting dresses, so they could pay a formal visit to friends and neighbors.[16] And then there were the doll funerals.

When Queen Victoria, ever the trendsetter, went into lifelong mourning over the loss of her husband, she sparked a period of romanticism over death and grieving. Funeral rites became ever more elaborate with grand processions, ornate headstones and mausoleums, and death portraits. These spectacular funerals were another way of publicly demonstrating a person's worth through material goods. Stages of mourning were long and divided into deep or full mourning, second mourning, and half mourning—each with corresponding clothing and etiquette. Dolls reflected these social trends with miniature mourning dresses and veils. Fathers were even known to build doll-sized coffins for their daughters, the way a dad might build a dollhouse for a kid today. This wasn't seen as morbid or disturbing. To the Victorians, death and grief were very much facts of life, and playtime was the chance to do a practice run before children endured the real thing.[17]

Bisque dolls reflected the fact that life was fragile and breakable and so were human bodies. For the upper classes, their bodies were treasured, protected, memorialized. For the working classes, their bodies were fractured, forgotten, disposed. These were the bodies that were used in doll assembly itself, considered just part of the machinery of mass production. And before the advent of labor laws, children were part of that toil. For the workers, physical effort led to aches, pin-pricked fingers, stiff backs, kiln-burned skin. But working-class bodies were also used as raw materials. Doll wigs were typically made from human hair bought from working-class girls.[18] In effect, this process made body parts from the working classes into a plaything of the upper classes.

This discomforting aspect of porcelain dolls might explain why there's a long-standing association between dolls and mortal fear. Killer dolls have been a fixture of the horror genre ever since faux fangs were paired with Transylvania. Chucky may be the most well-known murderous toy, but an exhaustive list of others has existed from 1936's *The Devil-Doll* to *The Twilight Zone*'s Talky Tina to 2014's *Annabelle*. Most attribute this creep component to one aspect—the uncanny valley. Journalist Linda Rodriguez McRobbie defines the term as "the idea that humans react favorably to humanoid figures until a point at which these figures become *too* human. At that point, the small differences between the human and the inhuman—maybe an awkward gait, an inability to use appropriate eye contact or speech patterns—become amplified to the point of discomfort, unease, disgust, and terror." In the case of dolls, McRobbie writes that the most lifelike ones are the ones that induce the most goosebumps, and "these are also the ones that have begun to decay in eerily inhuman ways."[19] But perhaps it's not merely the facsimile of a human body but the actual physical evidence of a body—human hair—that gives these dolls an eeriness.

And then there are Victorian grave dolls, which make the terror of Chucky look like, well, child's play. These were never playthings, but duplicates of deceased infants and children typically dressed in their clothes and threaded with their hair. Grave dolls would be displayed at the wake and later at the burial site. Like a death portrait, they were meant to present a flattering, loving picture of a lost child through a life-size double. But it's easy to look at these rites today and see Stephen King's next novel.

For myself, I saw porcelain dolls as merely pretty. But occasionally, tiptoeing past them to get to the bathroom at night, I'd have to convince myself that I was safe because my small-scale dolls lacked the leverage to hold a butcher knife. In the daylight, I'd laugh to myself, "I need to stop watching *Creepshow*. They're just dolls!" I wasn't ready to admit what made me afraid in those shadowy midnight moments: These dolls signified another life gone by.

* * *

Porcelain dolls had a counterpart: the rag doll. Where porcelain dolls were ornate, grandiloquent, and unyielding, rag dolls were simple, homey, and plush. This contrast was perfectly captured in the 1908 poem by Reynale Smith Pickering, "The New Christmas Doll Complains," where an elegant fashion doll can't measure up to a little girl's rag doll favorite.

> She never admires my curly gold hair,
> She doesn't rave over my eyes,
> She never looks twice at the clothes I wear,
> Nor is she impressed with my size.
> And all of her strange, supercilious ways
> Are especially hard to explain,
> When I see the affection she always displays
> For little old Raggedy Jane

Later the doll laments:

Oh, it's nice to be grand and all that, I suppose,
But of late I'm beginning to reap
The knowledge that happiness isn't fine clothes,
And that beauty is only skin deep.
So I wish that I wasn't so handsomely dressed;
I'd be glad to be homely and plain,
Could I change all my charms for the love that's possessed
By little old Raggedy Jane."[20]

There were two types of rag dolls. One was the homemade doll assembled from scraps. Throughout history, dolls have been made from discarded items—corn husks, wooden spoons, clothes pins, rags, even bones—the debris of life that could be repurposed to entertain a child when money was scarce. These were the playthings of working-class and enslaved children, that is, if they could manage to secure the materials or be allowed any time to play. The second type of rag doll was the commercial, expert-made rag doll, produced on a larger scale, mimicking the first category.

Because commercial rag dolls were bought by middle-class and even upper-class children, they offered a moment of class role-playing. Think of Marie Antoinette at Versailles impersonating a shepherdess with a flock of perfumed sheep. It's a sanitized, escapist view of the working class removed from any toil or hardship. Through the commercial rag doll, children could try on the humble simplicity of a homespun toy, with the option to discard it for more lavish ones if they chose.

Many commercial rag dolls were also stuffed with negative racial messages. As Robin Bernstein writes in *Racial Innocence,* "the cultural effort to objectify and later reobjectify African Americans found rich potential in doll play and doll literature, because all stories about sentient dolls reorganize the boundary between human and thing."[21] The Golliwog rag doll—a minstrel caricature with a dark face, broad red lips, and giant cartoon eyes—drew on the most damaging type of racist imagery. (The name itself became a racial slur in Britain where the character was first created.[22]) Raggedy Ann and Andy also drew from blackface imagery, Bernstein argues: "[Creator Johnny Gruelle] styled Raggedy Ann after the minstrelized role of the Scarecrow, as performed by the blackface star Fred Stone in L. Frank Baum's 1903 staged extravaganza."[23] Ann and Andy were also joined by a Black mammy rag doll called Beloved Belindy. And then there were the loaded Topsy-Turvy dolls, where two upper halves of a rag doll—one white and one black—are stitched together at the waist with a broad skirt—making a two-for-one toy. When the doll and skirt are flipped one way, it appears white, flipped back over, it appears Black. Another name for these dolls? "Topsy and Eva" after the characters in *Uncle Tom's Cabin* that had evolved into a vaudeville act. This nickname "[solidified] its link to the blackface-slapstick brand of entertainment," Julian K. Jarboe writes in *The Atlantic.*[24]

These toys reinforced the division of class and race and the understanding that certain children merited protection while others were dismissed and denied a childhood all together. As Bernstein writes, "angelic white children" were meant to contrast with depictions of Black children that were "so grotesque as to suggest that only white children were children." The function of these images was the "exclusion of Black youth from the category of childhood" and from the category of "innocent."[25]

Let's time hop quickly to the 1940s, when the watershed "doll test" was performed. Black psychologists Mamie and Kenneth Clark showed 253 Black children a set of dolls, identical apart from their coloring: two white, two Black. The children, ranging from three to seven years old, were asked which doll they wanted to play with, and then told to pick the "nice" doll and the "bad" doll. Most of the children opted to play with the white doll and linked it with positive traits. The Black doll was discarded and labeled inferior. These heartbreaking results, later used as evidence in *Brown v. Board of Education,* were proof-positive that Black children suffered from internalized racism caused by society's prejudice.[26] Golliwogs and their racist rag-doll kin were the poisoned well that had contaminated an entire community. Decades later, children were still feeling the sickening effects on their self-esteem.

Rewinding back to the late 1800s, it's evident there wasn't much consciousness around these issues. Victorians were a hardened lot that found discrimination and the abuse of children commonplace facts of life. Categorically, children of all races had little to no legal protections. But even Victorians' calloused hearts were softened by the case of Mary Ellen Wilson. In 1874, Wilson's New York State Supreme Court trial was "the perfect case of child abuse," according to Oneill's account in *Ungovernable*. This was because it involved "a pretty, white, nonimmigrant child who spoke clearly and humbly of her trials," which fell within the era's very limited definitions of a child worth saving. Ten-year-old Wilson wasn't just the image of the angelic Victorian girl, she also displayed the "right" level of abuse to inspire outrage: She was cut by scissors and bruised from blows, but she wasn't sexually abused, and that was critical—Wilson could still claim her "innocence." As unfair and horrid as it was, the mindset toward reported sexual abuse "would have made her story unpublishable and sullied her in the minds of the public . . . Would the adults feel it so important to save this Forlorn Innocent if she'd already lost her innocence?" Oneill asks.[27] Again, only the pure, angelic white child—the personification of a porcelain doll—was worth saving.

The public was riveted by Wilson's salacious story of abuse and redemption—it was the 1800s version of a viral moment. Wilson herself was rescued from a life of mistreatment and placed into a loving home—the angelic Victorian girl once again protected—but her case also established new child abuse laws that protected children on the whole, even those that weren't pretty, white, nonimmigrants. Toward the end of the 1870s, over 30 chapters of the Society of the Prevention of Cruelty to Children (SPCC) opened in the United States, and orphanages and other public institutions for the care and protection of children were put into place. That growing awareness also cast a hard light on child labor, especially around toys where the contrast was damning. The National Child Labor Committee called out the "unsanitary and unsafe" tenements where children were making dolls piece by piece. One pamphlet, "Dolly Dear" used a doll's perspective to view the world of the haves and have-nots, or in this case the play and play-nots:

Dolly, my dolly dear what did you see?
"I saw little children make dresses for me."
How old were these children when did they play?
"They don't play in that world, they work every day."
Dolly, but dolly, how long does that take?
"They nodded, we nodded, at night half awake."
Why didn't they feed you and take you to bed?
"The children who made me were often unfed."[28]

Even with this push toward reform, the class- and race-based discrepancies of the Victorian and the brief Edwardian eras were a chasm. What the working-class needed in the early 1900s was a flight of avenging angels.

What it got instead was Kewpies.

* * *

The story of Kewpies begins with cartoonist Rose O'Neill, a woman defiantly out of step with her era. Scholar Shelley Armitage describes her as "self-trained, twice-divorced, childless—a career-oriented creative woman in a male-dominated artistic world."[29] Accounts of O'Neill also call out her Titianesque beauty, legendary wit, good humor, and generosity. Her fanbase nicknamed her "the one Rose," highlighting her singular quality. Among the demure Victorian daisies, she was a wild, rambling bloom. But she described herself far more modestly as a "dynamic urchin," referencing her hard luck start to life. Her autobiography recounts acting out Shakespeare's plays in an earth-floored Nebraska cabin.

As an artist, she found tremendous success creating illustrations for magazines like *Puck* and *Ladies' Home Journal*. But her greatest triumph came when she doodled the cherubic, androgynous Kewpies in 1909. These Cupid knockoffs, with their buoyant bellies, dimpled cheeks, MoonPie eyes, and cowlicked hair, brought a sweetness and levity to the page. But more importantly, they expressed a concern for "women, the underclass, immigrants, and children," Armitage writes.[30]

Contrary to other cartoons at the time whose comedy punched down to the working poor, Kewpies used their humor to uplift the downtrodden. "Good behavior, fairness, cheerfulness, and community spirit are advocated in the Kewpies' actions, this moral sphere is achieved through a sprightliness that is neither predictable, autocratic, nor vengeful," Armitage notes. "Aspects of gender, race, and class are treated in egalitarian fashion."[31] In one cartoon, the Kewpies visit the Browns, a Black family who is struggling with racism and prejudice. After being rejected by white children, siblings Sam and Jasper Brown are transported by the Kewpies to a magical oceanside picnic complete with mermaids. In the final panel, Kewpies use their dumpling-like bodies to comfort the youngest child in an embrace. In another cartoon, the Kewpies find Jasper hiding in a barrel crying, and they present him with a Black Kewpie as a companion, a rare moment bestowing Black children with the same angelic innocence they were so often denied and implying a universal goodness among the young. Other adventures had the Kewpies protecting orphans, immigrant children, and neglected animals—essentially, society's most vulnerable.

This isn't to say O'Neill's illustrations weren't a commercial endeavor. Rotund Kewpies bubbled up around advertisements for Jell-O and Mansion House ice cream, but they also appeared on suffragist postcards and Red Cross announcements. O'Neill used her little fairy-elves as goodwill ambassadors in a mission to Kewpify the world.

Their wild success launched a fleet of Kewpie-themed products (plates, inkwells, wallpaper, ice cream molds), but none more cherished than the Kewpie doll. In 1913, German toy maker Kestner released the first bisque figurines with jointed arms, coy side-eyes, and a bright red heart in the center of its chest, signifying their love-fest approach to the world. They came with no trunk of clothes, in fact, no clothes at all. These little nudists were porcelain dolls with a conscience.

Given her own childhood, O'Neill was especially sensitive to her fans that were saving their pennies to participate in

Kewpie-mania. She instructed Kestner, "I want you to take the most care with the tiniest of the Kewpies, because those will be the Kewpies that poor children can afford to buy."[32]

Later versions were made in celluloid, composition, and plastic, which could be considered the ultimate compromise between porcelain and rags. Plastic offers all the durability of a rag doll, with the human-like appearance (hair, lashes, sleep eyes) of a porcelain doll. But it also suffers from the pitfalls of both of these materials. Like a rag doll, plastic feels common and disposable, and like porcelain, it can be stiff, hard, and unpleasant. So it follows that when Kewpies were reproduced in the 1960s and later, they were once again made in bisque, true to their original, angelic form. However, the modern versions are missing two critical things: the heart on their chest and the heart of their radically compassionate message. Divorced from their source material as protectors of the poor, Kewpies became just another generic cutesy baby doll.

The fact that porcelain dolls continue to be produced even today when so many more practical materials exist speaks to their ascribed value. These are the dolls we considered prized and worth preserving. These are the dolls that have survived a century later to populate our museums and auction houses. These were the childhoods we chose to protect and memorialize. They continue to act as a signifier for a person's class, whiteness, and European-ness.

* * *

I like to imagine the voyage of a single doll I owned: Her head was made in Armand Marseille's factory in Thuringia, Germany, a place that brings to mind cuckoo clocks and apple strudel. Her face, maybe one of 1,000 made that day, used the same numbered mold of all her sisters. That head would be strung together with a composition body, then she'd get her finishing touches—a cotton slip, a velvet dress, a ruffled hat, a wig of human hair. This particular doll was then bundled and exported. In my mind, I see her on a steamship headed off to Latin America. After a close call sailing around jagged Cape Horn, her crate sliding back and forth in the hull, she arrived in Santiago, Chile, where she was sold in a toy shop to an affluent family, perhaps European transplants themselves. Then more than 100 years later, while I visited my extended family there, I spotted her in a flea market laid out on a blanket. I was surprised to see her—*How did you get here, little one?* But I shouldn't have been. Anywhere there was European colonization, European toys followed.

This little doll had longevity, but her luck ran out when she was in my care. From her perch on my bureau, she took a tumble and cracked the back of her head. I screamed when I heard the thwack of porcelain meeting wood. My mother rushed in and reassured me—not all was lost. Together we took her not to a repair shop but to a specialized "doll hospital." It seems even with dolls, healthcare is limited to those with means. Here she was mended, because just like Mary Ellen Wilson, she was deemed worthy of saving when others—dolls, human beings—were not.

PLAY DATE #3

Who is she, our gal about town? Let's make up a backstory for our little doll. We know she came from the Victorian era, so we'll situate her then. But she's the heroine of our story, so she can't be a normal girl. Look at her: She's stunning! She's wealthy! Clearly, she's *somebody!* Clearly, she's *exceptional.*

I know what you're thinking: "Victorian lady? That comes with a lot of baggage. Didn't we just finish an entire chapter outlining how flawed the Victorians were? The things most Victorians believed about class, race, and gender would get you canceled today." Don't worry, our lady is progressive. She's marching for women's rights! She's championing science! She's super not racist!

Let's give her a few accessories to indicate that: a suffragette sign, a podium, a pamphlet of a speech by Sojourner Truth.

VOTES FOR WOMEN

AIN'T I A WOMAN

progressive

We could give her a friend, too, a sidekick who verifies her values. Her companion can be a scullery maid whom, despite their differences, she treats as her equal and BFF.

Historically, it's not accurate for a fancy lady and a scullery maid to have a deep, mutually respectful friendship—but that's nothing a flamboyant plot can't solve. A life-or-death moment of bonding should do the trick. What'll it be? Runaway horse carriage? Manor-house ghost? Five-alarm ballroom fire? Problem solved.

3 THE STORIES WE TELL

THE AMERICAN GIRL DOLL

As a little kid, I spent the holiday season arguing an air-tight case for my doll of the moment. I embellished my Christmas lists with little doodled hearts, rainbow stickers, even a yarn bow held on with Elmer's glue—all a blatant attempt to sway the jury of Mom and Dad.

I no longer spend the yuletide season shamelessly angling for dolls, but they still find me every December thanks to my mother's holiday ritual. Each year, she opens the lid of a painted trunk and unpacks her nativity collections, setting them out for display in her living room. These clusters of figurines come from various points in Latin America and use different materials and a variety of artistic styles to convey the same story in miniature: the birth of Christ. I have a favorite—a clay set from Mexico painted white and gold. Simple cone-shaped bodies and circular heads depict Mary, Joseph, and the rest of the ensemble, all topped with wire halos.

On Christmas Eve, we reenact the same tale. We remove the Jesusitos (baby Jesuses) from the sets, and at midnight, we ring bells, place them back in their crèche settings, and sing carols—*Christ is born!* It's a mini version of noche buena Catholic mass. At this moment, we are play-acting a narrative that has been passed down to me, to my mother, to her mother, and back through generations. The crèche collections become a mimeograph, cranked each and every year to make another impression.

What makes these figurines different from the wrapped doll under the Christmas tree? Not much. Throughout history, there has been little separation between an effigy and a doll, and frequently the same object would be used both for sacred rites and for playtime across cultures. One possible point of origin for the word "doll" is eidolon, the Greek word for "idol."[1] In 1544, the Canon of Bristol Cathedral, Roger Edgeworth, complained that people were taking figurines of saints and Madonnas from churches and giving them to children as playthings. Even for the craftsmen creating these items, there was overlap: The techniques used to make religious statues and crèches are the same ones that advanced European doll-making on the whole.[2] And then there is the similarity in purpose. Just like crèche figurines, dolls have been used as an educational tool to instruct children on rituals and retell history, often with an agenda.

That continued into the twentieth and twenty-first centuries. Folded into the larger fantasy of girlhood—the storybook princesses, fairies, and ballerinas—historical figures frequently pop up as a doll-theme. The midcentury toymaker A&H sold the flamboyantly named Dolls of Destiny line, which included representations of Marie Antoinette, Betsy Ross, and Martha Washington. Likewise, doll-maker Madame Alexander produced a series of first lady dolls in their inaugural gowns. Mini versions of Florence Nightingale and Mary Queen of Scots were among some of the other historic highlights the company made. Not to be outdone, Barbie rolled out toy versions of history-book mainstays like Amelia Earhart, Frida Kahlo, and even Rosa Parks as part of its "inspiring women" line in 2018. But these were all specialty lines in larger collections. Only one toy company jumped into the time machine with both feet.

* * *

In 1986, American Girl Doll launched with a novel approach: to make history the central selling point. The initial collection was just three dolls—Swedish prairie girl Kirsten, Edwardian-era New Yorker Samantha, and World War II tap-dancer Molly. These three girls represented three distinct eras (the 1850s, early 1900s, and 1940s) with the aim of giving an overview of American history at pivotal points for girls and women. Or more accurately, white women, as all three girls were white.

Even in its earliest days, American Girl was never solely about dolls. Part of their appeal was vibrant storytelling. Each character had her own line of books, documenting their grounded-in-history but nevertheless fictional biographies. These titles followed a six-book pattern that was repeated for each character (*Meet Kirsten; Kirsten Learns a Lesson; Kirsten's Surprise; Happy Birthday, Kirsten; Kirsten Saves the Day;* and *Changes for Kirsten*). Every book also closed out with the short essay "A Peek Into the Past," fleshing out elements of the story that connected to real historical moments.

To their credit, these stories did wrestle with important subjects, such as the classism and sexism of their time. But because they focused on their protagonists, all the stories centered on the white experience. Following the success of these three dolls, their manufacturer, Pleasant Company, expanded the collection in the '90s. The first addition was another white doll, Colonial-era Felicity. Then two dolls of color joined the lineup: Addy, a Black girl who escapes enslavement for a new life in Philadelphia, and Josefina, a Spanish-speaking girl from the early 1800s in what would become New Mexico.

The early collection serves as a bit of a personality test for young Gen X or older millennials. A Buzzfeed quiz on the subject pegs me as a Molly for being a "low-key nerd." But in my heart of hearts, I am a Samantha—fancy, girlie, sensitive. As a child, it was her books I checked out from the library and her catalog pages I studied in bed at night by flashlight. The turn-of-the-century trappings of her life—the miniature brass bed, steamer trunk, butterfly net— appealed to my love of Victoriana. I saw Samantha as heroic and cheered at her efforts to fight child labor in factories to save her impoverished friend Nellie. It never occurred to me to question whether Nellie's perspective wasn't the more relevant one, as the character that actually experienced those working conditions. (Nellie would have to wait until 2004 to get her own doll, part of the sidekick Best Friends line.) I also never questioned the absence of race in these stories and the way they echoed the dominant historical myths I received at school, instead of expanding my knowledge by telling stories that hadn't been widely heard before. In my playtime, I would reenact these stories, effectively repeating them and spreading their fictional, white-centered messages to other children as authoritative truth, and, of course, reinforcing them for myself, too.

I'm not the only one looking back at these texts to question them. Historians Allison Horrocks and Mary Mahoney have a podcast dedicated to revisiting these books with a critical eye. For Felicity's plot, in particular, one of a Virginia girl whose family owns enslaved people including plantation workers, the stories dodge any accountability for the main character and her family's exploitation. Early on in her narrative, Felicity risks "death by hanging" to liberate an abused horse. Yet, Horrocks and Mahoney argue, there's zero acknowledgment that she could have risked the same punishment to free an abused human being trapped in slavery. Throughout, enslaved people are only seen or mentioned at a distance, although their labor continues to benefit the family. "It's almost as if [the writer] wants us to take on the blinders that Felicity has as a child of privilege," Mahoney says. She sums up Felicity's attitude toward slavery as "I'm not really responsible for this, and I don't need to think about it," which in turn becomes the position of the reader.[3]

Here, I think of Monticello, the plantation home Thomas Jefferson designed and later lived in. Let's take a quick turn around its dining room. This buttercup yellow room was furnished with far more than engravings and fine China. Jefferson, ever the inventor, outfitted this room with dumbwaiters and gizmos, so a bottle of wine could materialize in a fireplace panel like a card trick. Historian Henry Wiencek writes: "Platters of hot food magically appeared on a revolving door fitted with shelves, and the used plates disappeared from sight on the same contrivance. Guests could not see or hear any of the activity, nor the links between the visible world and the invisible that magically produced Jefferson's abundance." Behind this system of levers and pulleys was not magic, as Wiencek explains, but the enslaved people of Monticello, sending up the wine and washing the dishes.[4] Jefferson knew that slavery could be distasteful to his guests and hurt his diplomatic efforts, so he concealed their toil within the walls of his home. This is the method American Girl uses with Felicity as well—the labor of enslaved people is hidden inside the walls of her story, but it's still the machinery that keeps these fictional households running.

This is the story Pleasant Company chose to tell. But children don't always follow the storyline when it comes to toys. A magic wand can become a lightsaber. The rubber duckie turns into a swamp monster. Couldn't Felicity also morph into something else? Through play, couldn't a child flip the script on Felicity to make the plantation girl the villain and enslaved people the heroes?

Theoretically, yes. But as I described, that would require an awareness of the humanity of those enslaved people, provided through narratives or even dolls. Of course, those dolls were never made; representation of enslaved people was sidelined in the books and totally absent in the catalogs. What *was* available for purchase were accessories that recreated the main characters' stories, such as Felicity's "Plantation Play" kit with a racket, a shuttlecock, and a whistle, among other items—showing the life of leisure she had at what many academics and historians now call "slave-labor camps," and inviting kids to participate in those same idle pursuits.[5]

Another reason it was unlikely that any child would give Felicity, or any of the dolls, the villain treatment was the issue of identification. As my Buzzfeed quiz indicates, fans of American Girl saw themselves as their doll, and that was by design. Along with books and accessories, Pleasant Company sold outfits where you could dress like your doll of choice, everything from pajamas to party dresses to tap-dancing costumes. Twinning was encouraged to emphasize that young girls from the past were not so different from young girls of today. You were encouraged to see yourself as the Felicity who loves horses and makes apple butter, not the Felicity who benefits from slave labor. Just imagine what a different narrative would have done to develop a child's compassion, awareness, and morality.

*　*　*

For a better understanding of American Girl's motives, it helps to hit rewind on the history of the toymaker itself. Pleasant Company was founded by former schoolteacher and textbook author Pleasant T. Rowland. On a visit to Colonial Williamsburg, Rowland had a light-bulb moment: a doll-plus-book-series bundle that could make history engaging for young girls. Rowland dodged the usual route of lining up investors and securing shelf space in toy stores after getting pushback that her vision lacked the price point and commercial appeal of toys like Cabbage Patch Kids. Her workaround? Using her own funds to launch a direct-to-consumer catalog. She recruited children's book author Valerie Tripp to write the accompanying novels. In 1998, shortly after Josefina was introduced as the sixth doll in the series, Rowland sold the company to Mattel where the series continued to expand past the initial six dolls, culminating with a total of 22 dolls from various eras. Mattel also grew other American Girl Doll lines that were divorced from the historical concept. But even today, the company emphasizes the book-doll connection, "We are not just makers of dolls or products, but we are storytellers," one promotional video explains.[6]

The seed money for Pleasant Company came from Rowland's textbook royalties.[7] While her work focused on reading, writing, and comprehension, it's very likely she was familiar with the power struggle taking place in her field over history, a push that resulted in publishers creating multiple versions of the same textbook to meet different state or district guidelines. One 2020 *New York Times* article summed up the blistering tug-o-war between red states and blue states that continues to escalate: "Conservatives have fought for schools to promote patriotism, highlight the influence of Christianity and celebrate the founding fathers . . . The left has pushed for students to encounter history more from the ground up than from the top down, with a focus on the experiences of marginalized groups such as enslaved people, women and Native Americans." According to the *Times'* side by side comparison, two textbooks from the same publisher—one for California, one for Texas—contain some stark contrasts. In one textbook, an excerpt from Julia Alvarez's *How the Garcia Girls Lost Their Accents* is replaced with a testimonial of a border patrol agent.[8]

Was Rowland simply a frustrated educator using these dolls and stories to sidestep a highly politicized system? Even possibly scout out a backdoor into classrooms, as the American Girl's teachers' guides imply? It's impossible to say for certain; Rowland is notoriously press-shy and has avoided interviews about her endeavors for years. But she was certainly hoping to publish books "where girls were the agent of change," according to Tripp.[9] My follow-up question would be, which girls exactly? As Mahoney and Horrocks discuss, these books don't just imply *what* American history is but also *who* it's for.

Rowland's post-Pleasant Company years are equally intriguing and knotty. Once she cashed out of the toy business, she used some of that capital to revitalize the town of Aurora, New York, which is on the National Register of Historic Places. Several of the residents protested that her renovations were not historically accurate and too cutesy. One resident complained, "The idea of stripping the interior of the Aurora Inn to put in a new interior that was 'faux-historic' was wrong-headed," inviting comparisons to American Girl's own manner of wallpapering over the bumpy surface of the past and making a dollhouse version of history.[10]

Still, when it came to creating Addy, American Girl's first Black doll, the company took great pains to get the story right. As Aisha Harris writes for *Slate*, "Rowland put together an advisory board of Black scholars and historians to advise on Addy's creation. This was an unusual step: While all the historical dolls had been developed with the help of outside consultants, Addy was the first doll to have a 'more formalized advisory board.'"[11] This A-team of experts included Lonnie Bunch, an established Smithsonian curator;

Janet Sims-Wood, a scholar at Howard University; and Violet Harris, an expert on Black children's literature, among others. It was their recommendation that Addy's story originate in slavery. They viewed Black American history as its own chapter book, one where the prologue had to be slavery in order to make sense of the pages that followed.

Addy's story, loosely based on the real life of self-emancipated Mary Walker, respectfully fictionalizes the horror of slavery and the bravery of escape. The veracity of every detail, from her cowrie-shell necklace to her fictional church in Philadelphia, was fact-checked by the committee. Despite all this careful consideration, Addy triggers strong reactions and debates online, especially with Black women who grew up with her. "I'm just now realizing that American Girl hustled me to buy a slave doll!!! Why was the only Black American Girl a legit slave!!!!" one person wrote on Twitter.[12] Others point to the jarring overlap between toy commerce and slave commerce. "I think I should sell my Addy American Girl doll. But I feel really weird putting an escaped slave doll up for auction on eBay," read another Tweet.[13] And yet, Addy advocates still defend her when disputes arise. "Calling Addy a 'slave doll' is so reductive . . . Spoken like someone who didn't read the books or know about AG dolls. . .#longliveAddy," replied another.[14]

Perhaps Pleasant Company's greatest failing was that it waited so long to release another Black doll. The team that worked on Addy envisioned this doll as a starting point, the first paving stone that would step toward other Black history moments, like the Harlem Renaissance. Doing so would give Black girls the opportunity to pick among a variety of characters and select the one that spoke to their personality, just as white girls were able to do. Unfortunately, for the first generation of American Girls, Addy was their only choice for representation. It wasn't until 2011—18 years later—that Mattel would release Cecile, a character set in 1800s New Orleans. And in 2016, the company launched the third Black historical doll, Melody, set during the Civil Rights era.

In its Mattel years, American Girl continued the Addy approach of recruiting a star lineup of historians, museum curators, and even linguists before launching dolls. For Kaya, the company's Native American doll, Mattel paired up with the Nez Perce tribe to verify every detail of her story and her appearance: her faux deerskin dress, her laced moccasins, even her smile. "She's the only American Girl doll without her two front teeth showing," Julia Rubin reports for *Racked*.[15] In the Nez Perce culture, showing your teeth is a sign of aggression, so Kaya lacks the chipmunk smile seen on all the other dolls in the lineup.

Kaya and Josefina (her New Mexican Spanish-speaking counterpart) capsize the Mayflower myth that America only began with East Coast pilgrims. And yet, their timelines feel suspect. As Emilie Zaslow notes in her book *Playing with America's Doll*, their stories conveniently take place before the conflict with white Americans (in 1764 and 1824, respectively). According to the company and their cultural consultants, they wanted to show these communities in a time when they were thriving—a worthy goal. But this omission side-steps any understanding or accountability of the Native American genocide for a white audience. Kids are invited to play with Kaya's teepee or Josefina's cross without learning about the racist, violent systems of oppression that put a chokehold on these cultures. Zaslow also notes that other white immigrant dolls, Kirsten and Rebecca, have moments of assimilation that makes them more familiar to the reader—going to school, pining after Hollywood movies—unlike Kaya and Josefina who remain outsiders and otherized.[16]

If there is a common thread among the characters, it's that every book tells the story of an Exceptional Girl. Buzzwords used across American Girl's catalogs include "spunky," "courageous," and "spirited." Their narratives celebrate individual liberation. History professor Marcia Chatelain finds the "endless exceptionalism" less than realistic: "The historian in me finds these 'girl power' narratives a bit grating," she writes. "Ultimately the books make clear that it is a single girl who makes the difference."[17] And it's the narrative itself, this girl-saves-the-day focus on the individual over the collective, that adds another racial blind spot to these books. As Koa Beck writes in *White Feminism*:

One of the prominent reasons white feminist ideology is well poised to step into a conqueror's narrative, and think nothing of it, is that their bedrock of empowerment is almost uniformly individualistic . . . A hallmark of many grassroots movements shunned by white feminism, across multiple and intersecting identities, is that they put forward collective rights before an individual's progress.[18]

Horrocks and Mahoney make this connection as well, nicknaming Felicity the "Sheryl Sandberg" of the series, referencing her book *Lean In,* a flashpoint of upper- and middle-class, capitalist, white feminism. "[Felicity] is 'leaning in' to what she wants. It's a very specific 'girl power' story," Horrocks says. "But she doesn't understand how she's leaning *on* other people to get it, like Marcus [an enslaved man in the novels]," Mahoney finishes.[19] That hardly matters to the Exceptional Girl; she has determined that "oppression is a temporary, individualized experience with personalized solutions."[20] And for the unexceptional, they simply aren't "spunky" or "courageous" enough to find society's loopholes.

Despite their shortcomings, these stories were wildly successful in one respect: They got girls interested in history. In my own childhood, history seemed like such a macho subject, full of war and conflict, founding fathers and explorers. One sagging bookshelf in my rec room had the complete set of *Time-Life*'s "Old West" book series. Illustrated covers showed Levi's-clad men racing on horseback, shooting in saloons, and fighting mountain lions barehanded (as one does). Even looking at their titles—*The Soldiers, The Frontiersmen, The Miners*—left little doubt whose life was considered worthy of note. American Girl expanded that testosterone-heavy definition by showing that domestic life, material goods—

that is, the lives of women—were also history. The beds, the hairbrushes, the dresses—these weren't just frippery but archival items, and that knowledge encouraged my interest in history and gave importance to my own life.

It's impossible to overstate how much these books could have contributed to a boom in women joining the field of history. At one point, Horrocks and Mahoney describe attending a panel for the National Council of Public History where the audience was asked to raise their hand if these American Girl books were important to their career path. Every hand in the room went up.

All this is why fans lament that the historical dolls are being displaced. Over the last decade, many of these dolls were "archived," and the accessories that accompanied these dolls, giving context for the character's material world, were discontinued. In effect, these dolls became less their characters and one more generic companion doll. The company shifted its focus and resources to its Truly Me line. Rubin writes, "[a]ll signs point to Truly Me's dominance, though American Girl would not confirm this."[21] But product placement in the store and the website do give plenty of confirmation, as prominent ground-floor and homepage spots are turned over to the newer line.

Who are these Truly Me usurpers? They are a somewhat customizable, build-a-bear-like concept for dolls where a girl can select the physical element of her toy through a spectrum of eye colors, hair colors, skin colors, along with details like glasses, wheelchairs, orthodontia, and more, creating the ultimate doll twin. For many kids and parents, this is the final victory of representation. "No one is left out—no race, no demographic. It appeals to everyone and that's something that we don't have much of today. For this to be able to appeal to each and every girl is pretty awesome," one mother raved.[22] Still, on a corporate level, it is far easier to simply dial up and down the pigment of a doll to increase representation than it is to devote a three-year cycle to researching the details of a specific historical experience.

These made-to-order dolls lack their own storylines, too; initially, they came with a set of six blank books where a girl could write their story—most likely her own, as the dolls were ready-made body-doubles—but even these books were soon discontinued. The company also releases an annual contemporary "Girl of the Year" doll, who has books set in the present day.

Much is lost with Truly Me and Girl of the Year dolls. While the power of seeing yourself reflected in toys shouldn't be dismissed, there is also power in knowing your origin story, or perhaps leaving the self-reflection behind completely and learning about someone else's experience divorced from your own—particularly if those stories come from marginalized groups. Even critics of the historical dolls see the Truly Me dolls as a poor replacement. "Alarmingly, the company appears far less concerned with telling the stories of girls in the past than it is with indulging girls in the present," Chatelain bemoans.[23] In an open letter in the *Washington Post*, Alexandra Petri is even more forceful in her criticism, relaying current plotlines for the Girl of the Year dolls that describe a life full of swimming pools, horseback riding, and golden retrievers: "Actual stories are being replaced with bland, featureless faces . . . Dolls Just Like Us. Is this really what we want? The image is embarrassing—privileged, comfortable. . . . No big adventures. No high stakes. All the rough edges are sanded off and the Real Dangers excluded."[24]

This points to an odd contradiction: On a tour of American Girl company headquarters, journalist Christopher Borrelli is told that the brand avoids politics, to the degree that they won't sell a doll with a water bottle, possibly because that indicates eco-activism.[25] Yet the historical dolls are often deeply engaged in the politics of the past, whether that's questioning segregation, imperial rule, or safe labor practices. In one of Melody's Civil Rights-era stories, she's told, "You are never too young or too old to stand for justice." It would follow that the contemporary versions of these characters would be equally active in their communities and engaged in the pursuit of justice, possibly joining Black Lives Matter protests or pushing for climate change regulations. Generation Z is a generation defined by activism—think of Greta Thunberg speaking at the UN, kids posting anti-racist TikTok videos—and yet, on these subjects, American Girl characters are mute. By emphasizing past activism while omitting its current counterpart, the company only endorses political positions that have long become the norm, and they push a conservative view that social issues like racism are a thing of the past.

This is why when the company announced in May 2021 that it was bringing back the original six dolls for a limited run, fans reacted with pure elation; to them, a hard-fought campaign to bring back Felicity, Kirsten, Molly, Samantha, Addy, and Josefina had been won.[26] And yet, as a lover of history and dolls, I wonder. Rather than simply reset back to the same six dolls and their same storylines, what would it look like if the company merged their two methods—taking a customized approach to historical variables the way they have for physical appearance? Horrocks and Mahoney attempt to do this using the tool of fan fiction. There is a good reason they turn to this medium as their outlet of redress. "[T]he vast majority of what we watch is from the male perspective—authored, directed, and filmed by men, and mostly straight white men at that," writer Elizabeth Minkel writes in her tribute to the genre. "Fan fiction gives women and other marginalized groups the chance to subvert that perspective, to fracture a story and recast it in her own way."[27] Their first attempt focused on Felicity's story, giving it a more satisfying ending and addressing some of the racial blind spots of previous books. Horrocks' invented tale flips the narrative, making Felicity's former rival, Annabelle, the protagonist. In her plot, Annabelle returns to her childhood home as an adult and buys the plantation from Felicity with the aim of setting all the enslaved people there free.[28]

Another attempt to customize American Girl's history can be spotted on the Instagram account @iamexcessivelydollverted, the account of public historian Rebekkah

Rubin who stages new scenarios for her American Girl Dolls, dressing them as Shirley Graham DuBois, Mary Church Terrell, and Anna Julia Cooper, among other real and imagined personas. Topics like temperance, the ERA, and the Chinese Exclusion Act are covered in the captions. "If you have a problem with your favorite dolls being political, maybe it's time to find a new hobby," she tells her followers bluntly.

Instead of intersecting history and customization, American Girl has chosen another crossroad, making a strange looping junction between past and present. One of their latest history dolls is Courtney, a 1980s white girl celebrating the technology and pop culture of the Me Decade. Though this move could be explained as a nostalgia-driven appeal to young mothers, something stranger is at play. By existing at the very time the original American Girl Dolls launched, Courtney situates the American Girl Dolls themselves within American cultural history, adding new weight to their authority. The American Girl Dolls are, in essence, mythologizing themselves as part of the American experience. Courtney herself owns a mini 1986 Molly doll and book, creating a cul-de-sac out of history. Or as one Tweet put it about the pairing, "History has caught up with itself. The cycle is complete. This Ouroboros has swallowed its own tail."[29]

* * *

About 10 years ago, I made an outing to American Girl Doll's 5th Avenue flagship store in New York City to celebrate my niece Erin's birthday. Beyond the revolving door was a multi-level bustling doll metropolis with a cafe, a hair salon, and a doll hospital. Fortified by a cafe lunch of mozzarella sticks and chocolate mousse where "Happy Birthday" was the constant soundtrack, we set out to explore our new wonderland. Some dolls were at the beauty parlor, getting intricate hairdos like French braids or space buns. Some were getting matching nail polish with their owners. Others were being outfitted with new gear, say earrings or purses shaped like puffed cupcakes. Rising and falling like a seesaw was the cooing and yelping of girlish glee.

"Oh my gosh! Oh my gosh! *Mom!* Look at these pajamas! *Doll pajamas!*" I heard one girl sing out.

At the tippy-top of all this was what could only be described as a mini-museum reminiscent of the Smithsonian's taxidermy dioramas. The squeals of previous rooms fell to a solemn hush as girls and their guardians filed past a series of vitrines, each with a historical doll. The wall text explained their dates and their backstory, treating each doll-like an ancient artifact.

Through this display, I see American Girl Doll solidifying its own unimpeachable sovereignty. *This is American history,* the room seemed to say in a booming movie-preview voice. And yet, and yet . . . As their very books have taught me— the dolls, their clothes, that room, the shop, even the girls squealing about pajamas—it was *all* history-in-the-making, every bit as valid as an Old West gunslinger and his trappings. Perhaps the very seriousness of that room was an attempt to spotlight and celebrate girl culture, when all too often it is swept under the floorboards of textbook footnotes. All I can hope is that as we build this history, we avoid constructing another Monticello—a monolith to white, individualistic values—and we knock a sledgehammer into the door frame, so it's wide enough for all girls to enter.

PLAY DATE #4

We've given our doll a wardrobe, a conscience, a companion. Let's give her an occupation. Not to worry, our lady isn't going to work in some factory, school, or secretarial pool. We're *playing*, not punching the clock. Her job has to be fun—the most fun imaginable. A job that requires oodles of beautiful gowns, a full calendar of grand events, and international attention. Shall we make her an actor? A singer? Some other performer? Whatever her talent, our girl is a star. Let's make her a stage as her backdrop.

This is where she can greet her hundreds of adoring fans. As the applause rains down on her, she can say sweet, modest things like, "You're too kind" or "Gracious! Thank you!" Perhaps she gives a deep curtsey to the floor, hand on her chest as roses are thrown over the stage lights.

When we get tired of enacting her success and all her curtain calls, we can play out her downfall. Give her a jealous lover, an opium addiction, a producer that pimps her out. Who doesn't love a shocking story of a damsel undone by fame?

4 HOW TO LIVE FOREVER

THE CELEBRITY DOLL

Tell me, who is your favorite Beatle? Your favorite Spice Girl? Are you a Marilyn or a Jackie? Team Aniston or Team Jolie?

When it comes to celebrities, many people treat them as a means to define their identity and divide into camps of competing fandom. I know I did. As a kid, I was firmly a Posh Spice girl—don't even try to tell me Ginger was better. I was also in Audrey Hepburn's camp, preferring the doe-eyed brunette over Hollywood's typical blonde bombshells. As a result, I had both their dolls, and I thought they said something about me, about my personality. I suppose they did to a degree. If you guessed that I was a prissy girl that loved old movies and bubble-gum pop songs, well, you'd be right.

But how much choice do celebrities really represent when it comes to identity, particularly for young girls? Stardom is limited to few, and even fewer celebrities get the doll treatment. Over time, something of a formula has developed for the stars we convert into dolls. They're the ones that have a set criteria we'd like little girls to absorb and reproduce, and they're an early lesson in the economics of feminine beauty and its shelf-life.

Our first celebrities were royals, and so too were our first celebrity dolls. Consider Japan's Hinamatsuri festival, which dates to the Edo period of the 17th century and continues today. This March 3rd celebration, also called "Girls' Day" or "Doll's Day," rolls out the red carpet for a full royal court in miniature. On a stepped platform blanketed in red cloth, various dolls are set out on display according to rank. The emperor and empress dolls preside over others on the top tier. The second tier is ladies of the court. Below that, male musicians, and on the fourth tier, ministers or bodyguards. The last tier is helpers or protectors, and any subsequent tiers hold toy-sized household goods (furniture, tea sets, tiny ox carts). These dolls are heirloom-quality objects and very pricey; often a family can only afford just a starter set of two. And that starter set is always the same pair: the royal couple, the most celebrated—and essential—of the group, both in doll form and in Edo society.

Europeans also gave their royals the doll treatment, especially Queen Victoria. "No doubt the happy combination of a young and pretty girl on the throne of a great kingdom, together with the great developments at the time in the art of wax doll-making, is responsible for it," Antonia Fraser writes in her historical overview on dolls. She notes that doll production for Victoria rocketed to the next level as she rose to power. "Some portrait dolls of Victoria as a young girl already existed before her accession . . . But the splendid coronation of the Queen produced a variety of reproductions of her image."[1] These elements—youth, beauty, accession— would all become key ingredients in the ideal celebrity doll.

Today, our celebrity worship is less focused on aristocracy. Instead, performers and movie actors occupy our top tier of fame. The 19th-century hype-monster and circus showman P.T. Barnum was part of that shift. In 1850, he did a full PR blitz on Swedish opera singer Jenny Lind, introducing her to American audiences. He rightly assumed that opera was a bit too foreign and lofty for the masses, so he billed her as a tender-hearted, altruistic singer with the moniker "The Swedish Nightingale."[2] The pairing of her angelic voice with this angelic persona was a smashing success, and Lind's likeness was reproduced in wax, China, and paper dolls. Lind's "good girl" character established a prototype for the type of star that would be dollified and distributed to little girls, one that upheld the values of sweetness, beauty, and humility.

The cheap thrills of paper dolls were also the perfect match for early movie madness. In 1919, famous silent-film actresses like Norma Talmadge and Elsie Ferguson were rendered in 2-D on the pages of *Photoplay,* an early movie-fan magazine, as a part of a paper dolls package. Off the printed page, silent-film actress Mary Pickford, the original

America's sweetheart, was one of the first to clone herself in doll form. Pickford excelled at playing the innocent, and as a 25-year-old woman, she was still cast as a child in *Poor Little Rich Girl* and *Sunnybrook Farm*.[3] Off-screen, Pickford was a savvy businesswoman who understood the cash crop a promotional doll could represent. But she struggled to find a good likeness, rejecting sixty different models before finally settling on a bisque winner sculpted by Christian von Schneidau.[4] Perhaps it was vanity, or perhaps image-conscious Pickford grasped the truth: These dolls would continue to be her cinematic body-double long after her acting career had ended. Pickford's "good girl" act also had a counterpart—Theda Bara, silent cinema's sultry bad girl. But Bara, who was nicknamed "The Vamp" and known for her revealing costumes and faux Egyptian background, wasn't a suitable subject for children. Only Pickford would be captured in porcelain and distributed as a doll role model.

While the Mary Pickford doll was a modest success, it couldn't touch the record-breaking mega-hit of the Shirley Temple doll—a tulip mania for the toy world. At just three years old, Shirley Temple was spotted in a Los Angeles dance studio, soft shoeing her way through a routine, her hair done up in ringlets. She was recruited in 1932 to star in a series of short one-reel films collectively called *Baby Burlesks*. Each one was a parody of typical movie genres—the newsroom drama, the rags-to-riches story, the Tarzan knockoff—but the parts were all played by children. Disturbingly, these efforts put toddler Temple in the stereotypical sex bomb roles of a nightclub singer, double-crossing honeypot, and bordello prostitute. At one point, Temple does a seductive dance in a diaper while toddler military men ogle her. *Burlesks* were not just exploitative, they failed to understand Temple's key appeal—her sweetness and innocence divorced from adult cares.

She hit a bull's-eye in 1934 with *Stand Up and Cheer!* In a case of art imitating life, the plot involves an effort to boost national morale during the Great Depression with a series of vaudeville acts. Midway through a ritzy song-and-dance number of chorus girls twirling, the screen fills with a set of puppet-dolls in ruffled dresses shuffling about. Then their ranks part, and Temple appears—the living doll—in a similarly ruffled dress. In this film, Temple finally gets to act her age, tap dancing and pulling on the coattails of her daddy who scoops her up for a kiss on the cheek to the crescendo of the song "Baby Take a Bow." It was this version of Temple, the star at her youngest just as the fuse to her explosive fame was lit, that Ideal Toy and Novelty Company chose to commodify in the very first Shirley Temple doll that same year.

Shirley Temple's subsequent movie roles could be summed up as human Kewpie, which is to say her mission was to lift up the downtrodden. Because it was the Great Depression, that included, well, everyone. The people-pleasing fantasy to be the world's greatest soother is one often pushed on young girls. It's not a fantasy of autonomy and adventure, but one of service. But there was power in playing this role. With unemployment at 25 percent and homelessness on the rise, there was an enormous need for soothing. And Temple delivered, whether singing about the bonbons of the "Good Ship Lollypop" or skipping up and down steps with Bill "Bojangles" Robinson. Even President Franklin D. Roosevelt came to see Temple's baby face and springy curls as an essential part of the country's recovery, dubbing her "Little Miss Miracle."[5]

At the time, movies were a public excursion, but the Shirley Temple doll allowed buyers to bring her brightness and light home. That offer proved irresistible. Even in the face of catastrophic economic hardship, Shirley Temple doll sales blasted off, accounting for about a third of all doll sales in 1935.[6] A key factor in the toy's tremendous success was that Temple was already dollified in her film roles. The titles and selling points of her movies—*Dimples, Curly Top, Bright Eyes*—were a catalog of her doll-like features. In dance numbers, she was often picked up and flung around like a plaything. And throughout, she was dressed in various baby-doll dresses with her hair set in ringlets. When rumors circulated that her corkscrew curls were actually a wig, fans would tug on her hair to test it for themselves, as if her real body was just another toy off the assembly line.[7]

That same public appetite for fame would keep expanding, blowing out the Hollywood spotlight and illuminating new corners of celebrity. In addition to fame achieved by talent (film stars) and fame associated by birth (royals), there was a third type of fame on the rise in the early 20th century: one that was media generated.[8] Though the Kardashians would have you believe they invented this category, the Dionne quintuplets beat them by about 70 years. Born in Ontario in 1934, these babies were the first quintuplets to survive infancy, which caused a media sensation. Like Temple, these little girls came to public awareness during the Depression, and they provided another much-needed dose of sweetness and hope. Various doll versions of the quints flooded the market, including a set by Madame Alexander that had five baby dolls in a bench-long rocker. By 1935, the Canadian government pushed through the Dionne Quintuplets Act, which officially made the girls Wards of the Crown until they were 18 years old on the premise that it would protect them from exploitation. But once under the government's care, the toddlers were moved into a nursery that became a major tourist attraction. Outfitted with a zoo-like enclosure the nursery drew approximately 3 million visitors from the girls' birth until 1943. In its heyday, Quintland, as it came to be called, rivaled Niagara Falls in its tourist visits.[9] The Dionne girls were an early forerunner of reality TV stars, living out their day-to-day lives for the entertainment of the masses.

The Quintuplet dolls and the Shirley Temple doll happened to hit the market when, thanks to radio and movies, vendors could speak directly to children and feed their fantasies. Before, toy companies had to appeal to parents via ads in publications like *Ladies Home Journal* or *Parents*, where they emphasized their educational or character-building qualities. But once a direct line to kids opened, the selling point was star power. "Hitch your product to a star," one toy buyer advised during the Depression as a way of avoiding price cuts. Kids buying these toys weren't just purchasing an object of play, they were purchasing a ticket on a flight of fancy.[10]

This success opened the modern era of the celebrity doll. Madame Alexander followed Ideal's footsteps by creating dolls out of movie stars like Jane Withers, Margaret O'Brien, and ice-skating-Olympian-turned-silver-screen-starlet Sonja Henie. While none of these were the smash-hit of Temple's, they kept the wheels of profit turning. Notably missing were any celebrity dolls of color. The casting in Hollywood's Golden Age pushed actresses of color into racist stereotypes, like Hattie McDaniel's maid and mammy roles or Anna May Wong's seductive Dragon Lady roles, which like Bara's vamp, were deemed unsuitable for children. It wasn't until the Civil Rights Movement that representation improved, and in 1969 Mattel released Julia, a doll version of Julia Baker, the prime-time TV character played by Black actor Diahann Carroll. While toy companies were very slow in depicting celebrities of color, they did reflect the emerging counterculture of the '60s and '70s through white icons like Twiggy and Cher. Today Barbie versions exist for a parade of red-carpet celebrities from Katy Perry to Heidi Klum to Zendaya.

Back when I bought my Audrey Hepburn doll, I wouldn't have been able to articulate what made her so compelling. Now I see how celebrity dolls offered something quite rare for girls—escape. Other girls' toys pushed the invisible labor of housekeeping and mothering. The Suzy Homemaker

Ovens, the toy Bissel carpet sweepers, the Betsy Wetsy dolls; they were all forecasting a future Betty Friedan would describe as "the problem that has no name." "There is no other way [a woman] can even dream about herself, except as her children's mother, her husband's wife," she writes in *The Feminine Mystique*.[11] On the other hand, "fantasy [toys] became equated with freedom" according to scholar Gary Cross.[12] And no one understood that more than young girls. With this freedom came a great amount of power. Even today, when women have more options apart from "homemaker," celebrity remains the brass ring of womanhood, the ultimate success that combines several desirable features into one powerful whole: bodily perfection, historical legacy, and upper-class advancement.

In the face of rising income disparity, class advancement has become even more enticing. Stardom and its enormous financial gains can be an escape pod launching from the 99 percent into the stratosphere of one-percent wealth. This is part of the Cinderella story we love to repeat—the grocery store cashier that became an Oscar winner, the waitress that now yachts in Cannes—because if they found an exit to inequality, we can, too. For women in particular, fame holds appeal as "modeling and acting remain two of the few fields where women can actually earn more than men."[13]

Celebrities also have something else frequently denied to young girls—visibility. In my school days in the 1990s, the study "How Schools Shortchange Girls" was released, documenting how boys were eight times more likely to call out answers in the classroom. When girls copied that approach, they were chastised and shushed.[14] The good girl is the quiet girl. This is why a pop star like Victoria Beckham was appealing to me. Not only was she heard, but she was blasted.

Yet as Temple illustrates, the divide between a human being and their doll doppelganger is never more porous than it is with a celebrity. Not only is the doll preserving the image of an idealized woman (or girl), but the woman is also rewarded for remaining in a doll-like state for as long as physically possible. In 2006, Temple (now Shirley Temple Black), was honored by the Screen Actors Guild with a Life Achievement Award. Dakota Fanning, then a child actor herself, presented the award with her own Shirley Temple doll in hand. "Even as Dakota Fanning gave life to Temple's greatest achievement—the Depression actress's performance of girlhood—she also marked Temple's greatest failure: the inability to remain a child," Robin Bernstein writes. "Of these effigies, only one will never grow and therefore never lose childhood. The doll, even more than Fanning or Temple Black, memorialized the doll-like perfection of Shirley Temple herself." Indeed, when the doll was reissued in 1957, Temple was nearly 30. Her truncated career was already over, but her doll self was ready to ride a wave of nostalgia on the Good Ship Lollypop.[15]

Likewise, Audrey Hepburn was still alive when I owned my doll version of her. She was in her sixties, working as a goodwill ambassador for UNICEF. As a child of war-torn Europe,

Hepburn had experienced starvation and desperation, and in her later years, she toured similarly devastated countries to raise awareness for their plight, especially to highlight its effects on children. Her efforts earned her the Presidential Medal of Freedom. But this accomplished sexagenarian wasn't rendered in plastic, even though her altruism would have made an excellent role model for children. Instead, my Hepburn doll was the cat-eyed coquette from *Breakfast at Tiffany's*. Hepburn in her UNICEF years no longer conformed to the formula of youth, beauty, accession.

It's this knife's edge of fame that Tavi Gevinson observes in an essay for *The Cut*. Youth and beauty, which are usually central to a girl's fame, are naively seen as a form of power, Gevinson explains. But this is a "deceitful notion" because this power is extracted from male desire and the male gaze. "This currency is not on your terms," she writes. "Even young women who are not megafamous have typically picked up on what makes them appear valuable by the age of 15. Their capacity to perpetuate these standards doesn't mean they are not also victims of these standards. If anything, it shows how girls' bodies and sexuality are so deeply regulated by a society that despises women and fetishizes youth that some of us learned how to carry out its work all on our own."[16]

The great escape I dreamed with Audrey—that powerful brass ring—can become a manacle, clamping down tighter and tighter.

*   *   *

Perhaps no one understood fame quite as well as Marie Tussaud—better known today as Madame Tussauds. Born in 1761, she found early success as an anatomical sculpture and portrait artist, until her profession got upended by the French Revolution. It was a rough start, but when life handed her lemons, she gave them a wax coating.

Tussaud began her career as an apprentice to a physician that made wax models for anatomy illustrations. She was blessed with two things: a keen business sense and a cast-iron stomach. In the 1780s, she used her skills to create wax portraits of the who's who—Voltaire, Jean-Jacques Rousseau. But when the French Revolution swung into full force, her work took a sharp turn toward the macabre. After her own close call with the guillotine for being a royal sympathizer, she found her new subjects—recently decapitated royalty. As Betsy Golden Kellem writes for *Atlas Obscura*, "The work required equal comfort in palaces and in prisons, and a certain ease with the grotesque."[17] Tussaud was quick to grasp that though life had left the faces of her new clients, fame certainly hadn't. "Even without their bodies, they were still the personalities of the time," Edward Carey notes in *The Guardian*.[18] Later, Tussaud would breathlessly recount balancing the head of Louis XVI in her lap while pressing wax into his face for a death mask.

Eventually, the revolution and its aftermath drove Tussaud to seek her fortunes elsewhere, and she made her way to England with "a duffel bag of disembodied aristocratic wax heads," according to Kellem.[19] It's here that Tussaud mounted a traveling exhibition of life-size celebrity dolls, finally setting up a permanent location on Baker Street in London. (The apostrophe was eventually dropped from the name Tussaud's, making the establishment's official name Madame Tussauds.)

Carey reflects on those first spellbound audiences: "Imagine how extraordinary it was for a Londoner in the early 1800s to be shown exact replicas of famous faces of the time. Here, [Marie Tussaud] said, is history. And she related her own role in it to fascinated audiences: She had lived at Versailles, been art tutor to Louis XVI's sister and cast the king from life." It was that proximity to fame that made Tussaud's figurines so compelling. "Anyone could make a diorama, but only Marie Tussaud could claim she had taken her casts from the very individuals portrayed."[20]

For Tussaud, every kind of fame was fair game. Marie Antoinette was on display, but so were the notorious body-snatchers and murderers William Burke and William Hare. Her view on celebrity was best summed up by her two chambers: the Golden Chamber, where the public could crowd in next to a reproduction of Queen Victoria's wedding, and the Chamber of Horrors, where gruesome executions were staged. "Madame Marie knew that the public, then as now, would go nuts for two things—royal fever and horror shows," Kellem writes, "and she gladly provided immersion in both."[21]

Just as with their toy counterparts, Madame Tussauds' life-size wax dolls grew to expand their definition of celebrity in subsequent years. Today, red-carpet actors like Nicole Kidman take priority, and current rooms in the Los Angeles outpost include A-list Party, Pop Icons, and Spirit of Hollywood themes. There is a reason that, long after photography has made celebrity images readily available at a click or a tap, the public continues to come to wax museums. Part of it is the physicality: "We want to know the precise amount of space that Marie Antoinette took up, and to know what her head looked like after it was cut off," Carey maintains.[22] But part of it is insight into what makes fame appealing. "Marie Tussaud was a hustler," Kellem writes. "[She created] what we recognize as the modern concept of celebrity—renown not being something you achieve after death with a sober legacy, but something you cultivate in life by slaking the public thirst."[23]

Carey touches on the fact that not everyone came to Madame Tussauds for celebrity worship. "It was often disturbing to see how real people behaved in front of the wax people. In the end you had to conclude that the wax people had more dignity." This makes sense: Our feelings toward celebrities aren't pure. They're muddled with power inequalities that affect our own lives. Much like the French revolutionaries who reveled in toppling royalty, the public feeds off a specific brand of schadenfreude when celebrities are brought low. One small aspect of this can be seen in the gleeful articles about ugly celebrity dolls that went awry: "11 Hilariously Bad Dolls That Look Nothing Like the Celebrities They're Modeled After" or "16 Celeb Dolls That

Are So Bad They Will Make You Cry."[24,25] These roundups echo the same tone tabloids take when documenting Hollywood plastic surgery gone wrong. If beauty is capital, then these stories are cheering for someone's bankruptcy. But then, seeing the mighty dragged to the poorhouse was entertainment in Tussaud's time and now, too.

Losing face, literally or figuratively, isn't the worst fate of a female celebrity. The outcome can be far more bleak. Karina Longworth's Hollywood-themed podcast *You Must Remember This* has a 13-part series simply titled "Dead Blondes." As the name suggests, it chronicles the bad end for various starlets from Jean Harlow and Marilyn Monroe to Peg Entwistle and Barbara Loden.[26] This series reminds me of a particular scene from the 2010 movie *Beginners*. In it, aspiring actor Anna is rummaging through a used bookstore with her love interest Oliver. They thumb through a book about Hollywood lore together. Oliver summarizes the final chapter of various female performers, "She was a pin-up model and a film star . . . success was short-lived. A series of broken marriages . . . She struggled with mental illness and alcoholism . . . " Anna cuts him off, "All these actors' stories end sad. I can tell you that already."[27] And often that end is both sad and violent.

This aspect—the bad end of an attractive, successful woman—is a common form of doll play. Violent play-acting through dolls, particularly Barbie dolls, is well documented. "I just found it fun to cut off all of Barbie's hair and perch her on a window. Before I shoved her off," one woman recalled.[28]

"I asked for Barbie dolls, but then mutilated the ones my mother grudgingly bought for me—until she stopped buying them," another reveals.[29] *Jezebel* staffers even go so far as to attempt to electrocute Barbie in a homemade electric chair.[30] Writer Tanya Lee Stone theorizes that this doll-abuse comes from jealousy, but I see it as a reenactment of the dominant story we tell for beautiful, celebrated women, which often has a tragic, violent third act. In this way, through our dolls, we are still visiting Madame Tussauds Chamber of Horrors. The result? Another dead blonde—this time Barbie.

But just as Tussaud recognized, death doesn't end celebrity—in fact, it can spotlight it. After Princess Diana died in 1997, the production of collectible dolls in her likeness reached an all-time high.[31] However, some aspects of celebrity have changed since Tussaud's time. Social media has atomized fame, dispersing droplets of followers by the 100K to various internet personalities. Here the aim is to "be your own brand" and fabricate a fantasy life of perfectly stylized, manicured vignettes—little dollhouse moments—to gain followers and influence. In other words, to obtain fame. Jia Tolentino describes this new social media starlet in depth:

She's got glossy hair and the clean, shameless expression of a person who believes she was made to be looked at. She is often luxuriating when you see her—on remote beaches, under stars in the desert, across a carefully styled table, surrounded by beautiful possessions or photogenic friends. Showcasing herself at leisure is either the bulk of her work or an essential part of it . . . Can you see this woman yet? She looks like an Instagram—which is to say, an ordinary woman reproducing the lessons of the marketplace, which is how an ordinary woman evolves into an ideal.[32]

In effect, social media—like movie screens, like dolls—has become yet another surface to beam the image of the ideal woman and to tell girls: *Strive for this.* The difference is social media offers fame at warp speed. Andy Warhol's proverbial 15 minutes has been shortened to a tight 60 seconds on TikTok, and by its nature, these moments are single-use and disposable.

There is a great deal of effort in producing these images, an effort to optimize the physical self, which can either take place behind the scenes or be documented as an empowering choice for self-care that followers can imitate. Successfully reproducing this image is a monetizable skill that reaffirms a woman's status "as an interesting subject, a worthy object, a self-generating spectacle with a viewership attached," Tolentino writes.[33] Once again, this elevated status becomes the brass ring of womanhood. And once again, the empowerment offered is not true power because it's dependent on the male gaze and unforgiving beauty standards.

Just as the silent-screen queens had their paper dolls, these new celebrities have even been dollified to capitalize on this new form of fame while reinforcing its standards. #Snapstar dolls, which come in boxes resembling an iPhone, have the tagline "Do cool things, take cool photos." According to one toy site, "Each #SNAPSTAR includes a doll that comes with a full outfit and accessories, a removable hairstyle, a green screen, a stand, and of course, a doll cell phone because what's an influencer without their digital lifeline to the world?" Using these toys, girls can work on perfecting, as Tolentino puts it, "the tools that will allow her to look more appealing, to be even more endlessly presentable, to wring as much value out of her particular position as she can."[34]

*   *   *

"Cafe latte from The Roast!" reads the caption. The image is a brunette in gold hoop earrings, patterned tights, a leather skirt, and a chunky sweater. Her trench coat is hanging off her shoulder *just so*. In her hand is a takeaway coffee cup, and next to her sits a little French bulldog. But the subject here isn't a person, it's a Barbie-esque fashion doll called Poppy Parker on the account @dolliberate.

I'm scrolling through Instagram on my phone. It's mid-afternoon and I'm groggy, slurping my fourth cup of tea for the day. This is time I've put aside for frolicking through candy-colored apps before I get back to work. When I tap on the sherbet square of Instagram, I see an endless scroll of doll-themed accounts I follow from users like @dolliberate and @escapefromtoybox, @barbielifeinthevilla, and @daintydolldivas. These dolls are jamming out on keyboards, sitting in lotus pose, swapping around their home decor, running out for a donut, surfing in Malibu—in short, they are living their best lives with captions like "Hang Ten, Honey," next to plugs for Patreon accounts, Etsy shops, and affiliate links.

The caffeine isn't doing its job, and the images swim before me, a lapping wave of pouty faces, coiffed hair, and exposed midriffs. For a suspended moment, I forget that these aren't real girls. They look like the feed of every influencer: a glossy, studied casualness. But then, who can say what's *real*. Here is a doll that is pretending to be a girl that is pretending to be a doll. The images begin to shimmer like a mirage.

I'm reminded of a toy from the 1800s called a thaumatrope, a cardboard circle on a wound string with two images on either side. One common version has a bird on one side and a cage on the other. When the disk spins quickly, an optical illusion shows the image as one: The bird is in the cage. Just like that old trick, I see these two images—the doll and the girl—layered on top of each other, merged, and caged.

I've had enough. I close Instagram. Its camera icon resembles a single eyeball, staring back.

PLAY DATE #5

If you've been reading this as an e-book, our paper doll is merely a figure on a screen. But that doesn't mean we can't still play with her. In fact, this could be the most appropriate place to have our play date. After all, digital spaces are where we turn for most of our entertainment these days: the TikToks, the Tweets, the Animal Crossings.

On an e-reader, our doll is just a collection of pixels. But aren't we all speckled dots when we're on screen? Here, this stippling of dots is a doll, just as this other cluster of dots is me on Facebook, and this other set of dots is me on Zoom.

When everything is virtual, it's all made from the same pixelated stardust. Online, there's no difference between me and this doll.

Offline, however, is another story.

5 VIRTUAL PROXY

THE AVATAR "DOLL"

bitmojis

By now, you may have a mental image of me as a child. Perhaps you see me as someone who wore lace granny dresses, lifted her pinky to drink orange juice, and used words like "indubitably." Doll lovers can be pegged as girlie, fussy people. And certainly, part of me fits the mold. But I was also just a kid in the '80s and '90s, participating in the pop culture fads of those decades. I went to roller-skating rinks and McDonald's ball pits and arcades for endless rounds of *Centipede* and *Q*bert*. I never had great dexterity, button-mashing my way through levels, but I did my best on my family's Atari, which later gave way to a Nintendo. And I have happy memories of playing desktop games like *Ultima* or *King's Quest*, tap-tapping the arrow keys across a pixelated Medieval Europe.

That first wave of childhood games became a global tsunami of Mario Bros.-style platformers, garage-band simulations, first-person shooters, Candy-Crushing apps,

Zelda-type quests, multiplayer battles, sports, puzzles, and on and on, eventually with YouTube and Twitch accounts to document it all. More and more, our physical objects of entertainment are going digital. And dolls, too, have their digital counterparts.

One early effort to market video games to girls and center their interests was the CD-ROM game *Barbie Fashion Designer*. Essentially, it was a souped-up, on-screen version of paper dolls. Players designed themed outfits for Barbie ("Totally Trendy!" and "Dream Date!" for example) altering their cut, color, and fabric pattern from a set template. Then Barbie could model the finished design to a jazzy synth soundtrack, or kids could print out their runway efforts. *Fashion Designer* was a hit, outselling some of the most popular games of 1996. Eager to capitalize on this new audience, several Barbie-themed games followed: *Barbie Magic Hair Styler*, *Barbie Nail Designer*, *Barbie Riding Club*, *Barbie: Magic Genie Adventure*, and so on.

American Girl also teleported their dolls and books into a desktop game. In *The American Girls Premiere*, gamers could script "plays" for the historical characters and then watch those stories acted out by animated versions of the books' characters on a red-curtained stage. One shortcoming was the "horrific, computerized voices" of the characters according to one reviewer, who uses the robotic delivery as a punchline by writing a script where Felicity and her father say a prayer in binary, "01100101 0111011001100001 01101110. Amen."[1] American Girl's digital efforts continued under Mattel: They later launched *Innerstar University* that built "a bridge between the contemporary doll a girl owns and the online world where she is spending more time," a company spokesperson told the *New Yorker*. "When a girl buys a [doll], she gets an access code to 'enroll' her doll online," Adrienne Raphel writes. "The online versions of the physical dolls can be homework buddies, dance at U-Shine Hall, get streaks in their hair at the Real Bright Salon. You can communicate with fellow Innerstars through a pre-written set of messages."[2]

Despite being a doll nut and a gamer, I was never drawn to these specific games. Part of the issue was they didn't seem to mimic my actual doll play, which was as much about interaction as it was about outfit changes. *Innerstar* seems to come the closest, but this virtual campus was shuttered in 2015, perhaps for good reason. "To play doll yoga," Raphel explains "you slowly trace your mouse over the doll as she goes through sun salutations. It's as exciting as it sounds."[3]

But virtual dolls are everywhere online if you look for them—not by name, but by one of their primary functions: Acting as a proxy for the idealized self.

Many toy manufacturers, including American Girl Doll, allow children to create a plush or plastic avatar. Kids pick their toy's eye color, hair color, and skin color to match them, creating a companion doll that represents a mini-me. This exact process is mirrored in the digital world with Bitmoji. Users select the haircut, glasses, freckles, etc. that represent their personhood, although physically these representations are still fairly homogeneous (try finding a Bitmoji with acne or an underbite). Ultimately this self-expression is still limited to a tech company's predetermined checklist of physical attributes.

About five years ago, I created my own Bitmoji—a dimpled brunette doppelganger that I'd text to friends while making social plans. "Let's get tacos!" she'd announce. Or, "Pajama party time!" Or, "Netflixing my life away!" More than any video game, these text exchanges come the closest to recreating my childhood doll play. As a kid, when I sat at the kitchen table and announced to my mother that my doll Sonia wanted Cheerios for breakfast, I was expressing my desires behind the safety of a Cabbage Patch mouthpiece.

And Bitmojis aren't the only alternate selves available to the technologically savvy. Avatars are everywhere. A few years ago, I watched in fascination as my nephew Will played *NBA 2K,* an Xbox game. Here's what I expected to see: players on a basketball court dribbling and dunking as a faux commentator shouted things like, "He's on fire!" or "Boomshakalaka!" Those were the sports games of my youth, the *NBA Jams* and the *Double Dribble* of the arcade world. Here's what I saw instead: a wall of physical variables—hairline, skin color, facial hair, jawline, eyes. Will was assembling his character from a menu. Then came the clothes, the shoes, and finally the publicity photo shoot, all before the opening tip. In shock, I recognized this preamble. It was a paper doll for the *NBA 2K* set.

On the more fantastical side of things, there's *Second Life*. Unlike many video games, this virtual world has no endpoint and no set objective. Users can mill around, explore, and socialize just as they would in a tangible space. There are few limitations on *Second Life* avatars. Users can add custom, "mesh" overlays to the standard avatars, often paying third-party designers for tailored attributes like specific skin or clothing, or characters in the style of *Star Wars*, *Dragon Ball Z*, or other fantasy realms. One site advertises its creations piecemeal, with a price list breaking out furry additions like "fox ears," "little horns," or even full shark getups that arguably represent the user and their interests better than their physical body.

In the *New York Times Magazine*, Amanda Hess takes inventory of the avatars she's created, the various virtual selves, for different spaces:

> On Facebook, I'm posed by a professional photographer, waist contorted into a slimmed line, eyes peering up out the window of a skyscraper. On Snapchat, I'm burrowed into my office chair, blankly blinking my eyes open and closed. On Candy Crush, I'm a cartoon man-otter. I don't particularly know why I've selected these avatars as my representatives; it's some combination of my read on the platform's sensibility, my emotional state at the time of upload, and the suite of photos I had on my phone at that moment.[4]

Hess's last example highlights the fact that photos can act as avatars, especially those that have been manipulated with filters, cropping, retouching, etc.

In recent years, every digital space and medium is getting avatar-ized. Not long ago, my emails were nothing but a box around a string of words. But now that little box comes topped with a ponytailed girl wearing a Mona Lisa smile. This is my headshot and my Gmail avatar. The text that follows, once the sole content of the message, could be read as a speech-bubble coming from her pink lips. Once again, I'm expressing my desires ("Sonia wants Cheerios for breakfast") through a mouthpiece. Likewise, my article bylines for various media outlets used to be my name alone, but recent website redesigns mean my name is now accompanied by my headshot. My thoughts do not stand on their own, they have a ponytailed tagalong.

Avatars are also changing the function of our digital tools, like emojis. Ian Bogost writes in *The Atlantic* that emojis were once a suggested object, "like airport signage." A snowman wasn't a literal snowman. It could signal chilly weather or "a gripe about the office thermostat." But "over time, the visual language has shifted away from abstract, ideographic uses and toward specific, illustrative ones."[5] And that includes depictions of the people in emojis. No longer are a set of prayer hands meant to indicate your hopes and prayers or gratitude, but also your own two palms pressed together. For this reason, there's been a demand for more skin color, hair color, and eye color options. It's a wonderful step in the right direction for representation, but demanding an exact duplicate of ours and others' physiques can cause headaches. Studying the "family" emoji, a cluster of four people in a pod,

Bogost writes, "Adding different skin-tone options for each family member in multi-person groups . . . would result in 4,225 permutations." What we are asking for is a galaxy of avatars.

*　*　*

The word "avatar" has become so deeply linked to our virtual presence—and a certain James Cameron movie franchise—that it's hard to remember that for centuries, it was part of a spiritual vocabulary, not a technological one. Originally a Sanskrit word meaning "descent," avatar describes the moment when a Hindu god came to earth and took a mortal form. "In Hindu theology," Hess writes, "Vishnu assumes various earthbound avatars—among them a fish; a tortoise; a half-man, half-lion—in an effort to restore order at times when humanity has descended into chaos."[6]

The word avatar was copy-pasted onto gaming precisely because it was a tool to encourage our better angels. As Hess notes, "Richard Garriott, creator of the Ultima games, said he came across the Hindu concept while looking for a way to encourage moral behavior in gaming. He was disturbed by players who took the easiest possible route to win the game . . . So Garriott started framing his hero as an 'avatar' instead of a 'character.'"[7]

Garriott's approach worked. Stanford researchers Jeremy Bailenson and Nick Yee proved a person's behavior could be swayed significantly both online and in real life by their avatar, something dubbed "the Proteus effect." For example, when gamers were given a more attractive avatar, they behaved in a more confident manner. That influence becomes stronger and stronger when the avatar resembles them as opposed to a generic-looking figure, according to Jesse Fox, another scholar studying these connections. Avatars allow people to do a trial run on real-life interactions. "They allow us to practice and test out certain behaviors in a virtual world," Fox told the *New York Times*.[8]

But what is a "real-life interaction"? In recent years, the gauzy division between the real world and a virtual one became as thin and permeable as single-ply Kleenex, especially following 2020, a year when our digital world became our primary one. In this shift, kids are leading the way.

During the pandemic, playgrounds in the physical world closed, but the sandboxes of *Minecraft* and *Roblox* were more crowded than ever. Of the latter, the *New York Times* reports, "[a]bout three quarters of American children ages 9 to 12 are now on the platform . . . And players spent 3 billion hours on the site [in one month]."[9]

The classroom went through a similar transition. Struggling with Zoom fatigue, many teachers turned to Bitmoji to help with engagement. One site, *Education Week*, covered the craze: "Bitmoji classrooms are becoming a teacher obsession," Catherine Gewertz writes. "With technology, teachers can try to recreate a version of one of their most cherished traditions: building a colorful, comfortable, and personal space for the new faces that cluster in front of them each fall."[10]

In these spaces, real and digital worlds are one. The friends you visit in *Minecraft* are your "real" friends. The assignment your Bitmoji teacher gives you is your "real" homework. In this new reality, the philosophy of selfhood could be, "I log in, therefore I am." In fact, for this next generation, digital representations have replaced physical ones as the ultimate affirmation of existence. Take this book as an example. If no record of it appeared on Amazon, would you still be confident that what you held is a published book? Or would you begin to wonder if this wasn't just a collection of pages printed and glued together?

No one understands this shift more than the gaming couples who meet, date, and marry in virtual spaces, or as writer Stephanie Rosenbloom put it, the ones who found "love at first kill." Among these couples, it's not uncommon for them to host a wedding for their avatars. When asked why multiplayer love connections are so common, one gamer put it this way: "When you're talking on the phone you can say [romantic] things, but there's no physicality to it. And in the game, even though somebody's 2,000 miles away, they've made an effort to sit down and hold your hand."[11] Here the phone lacks a physical dimension, but the game does not. Sitting and holding hands through a controller is "real," even if you can't actually feel the warm contact of their touch.

In addition to these happily ever after endings, so much good has come from people being able to select an authentic physical self in these realms. Not only does it affirm bodies that come in a wide range of skin tones, shapes, and abilities, but it also supports the exploration of sexuality and gender. Laura Parker wrote about the positive effect *The Sims* had for Dr. Robert Schloss, a formerly closeted shipboard physician in the United States Navy Medical Corps. After Schloss made two same-sex couples in the game and played house with them, he realized gay domestic bliss was what he wanted for himself. Likewise, a patch for *The Sims* in 2016 erased gender limitations on character creation. This allowed Blair Durkee, a trans woman, to assemble a character with features like her own—a slim redhead with broad shoulders and a deep voice. "When I was younger, I always wanted to play games as a female character, even before I knew why," she tells Parker. "I can't fathom how different my life would be if I were exposed to positive representation of trans people at a young age."[12]

But there is a strong moral streak around conforming to your avatar. A resemblance between you and your virtual self is expected. If there's a disconnect, it's treated as a deception—or worse.

In a nostalgic tone, Hess writes about the early days of avatars: "In discrete gaming worlds, value systems were strangely authentic: Everyone was building his or her mini-me in the same system and playing by the same rules." The breakdown, according to Hess, is when "avatars became ambiguous." "Bad actors could sulk under the cover of the Web while they pasted reputation-killing content on a message board or terrifying threats on Twitter. Avatars became tools for stoking chaos instead of enforcing order."[13] Here, the good virtual citizens are ones that create mini-me avatars. The lawbreaking agents of chaos and fear are the nonconformists that have no resemblance to their virtual selves. Anonymous, the anti-establishment hacker group who hides behind Guy Fawkes masks, are one classic example.

At times, this moralizing seems appropriate. During Black Lives Matter protests on *Roblox*, the *New York Times* reported that several users participated but darkened their avatars' skin color, presumably in a misguided attempt at solidarity. Garvey Mortley, a twelve-year-old Black user, rightly calls it out as a case of "virtual blackface."[14] This type of racial appropriation also happens with emojis. Seeking advice from the podcast *Code Switch*, a mother asks how to discuss race with her daughter, a 15-year-old white girl who uses Black hand emojis. Kumari Devarajan replies:

When we step into the digital world, it's easy to feel like we can leave our IRL identities behind. But the power dynamics that exist in real life don't disappear just because we're hidden behind a screen . . . Does she think her raised-fist emoji looks more revolutionary when she paints it black? Her clapping hands more rhythmic? Her praise hands more dramatic? Her painted nails sexier? If that turns out to be the case, then you should explain to her that she is playing up harmful stereotypes about black people, even if that is not her intent.[15]

Yet for women in particular, the pressure to present as avatar-perfect, and the moral failing if there is a mismatch creates a new suffocating beauty standard.

Take my Gmail avatar for example. This headshot was from a package of wedding photos. I had paid a professional photographer and a makeup artist. I was posed on museum steps in soft lighting; it was a good hair day, and I was coached to smile in a way that created the perfect Doll Face. She is me, but she's a manufactured version of me. This image was purchased, the same way *Second Life* users can purchase a custom avatar. Now, she is the face people see when they contact me. If someone I emailed—a potential employer, a landlord, a loan officer—were to meet me in real life and find a chasm between this avatar and the real woman before them, would they feel duped? Question my honesty? And what could it cost me?

Back in Airbnb's early days, I created an account using a screenshot of LOLcat legend Grumpy Cat as my profile picture. When I attempted to book a listing for a weekend getaway, my booking was rejected. The owner direct messaged me to let me know that while my credit card went through, it was my avatar he declined. "I like cats," he wrote, "and I'm sure your picture is meant as something funny/playful. But what I'd like to see is a picture of the potential guest, not their pet." Chastised, I switched out this whiskered frown for a smiling snapshot, and my next booking was confirmed. But I have to wonder: why exactly did this man feel entitled to a photo of me, and what did he need to confirm? Did he need to assess my attractiveness? My race? My age? My basic humanity?

There is a deep-rooted fear around shape-shifting women, one that goes all the way back to ancient mythology, the bedrock of Western culture. In *Women and Other Monsters*, Jess Zimmerman makes the argument that our original scary stories—Medusa, the furies, sirens—are still with us, casting their long-tailed shadows onto women, even today. For men, these O.G. monsters brew "a suspicion of women in general, a feeling that every one of them may have claws and tails if you look below the waterline."[16] The murkiness of the internet brings these old fears bubbling back to the surface. One such swamp thing is Scylla. Ovid describes her as a beautiful nymph from the waist up, but below the belt, her body is a pack of snarling dog heads, capable of ripping into a man like he's a bucket of Kentucky Fried Chicken.

Yet like beauty, monstrousness is in the eye of the beholder. Zimmerman writes,

> If the expectations are too narrow, nearly anything can become monstrous. If you are only allowed to be tiny, it is grotesque to be medium. If you are only allowed to be quiet, it is freakish to be loud. The more you are circumscribed, the easier it is to deviate, and the more deviation comes to seem outlandish or even dangerous.

Scylla's particular myth, she argues, is actually about exposing a woman's body as flawed simply because it can't maintain a fantasy indefinitely—even the sexiest supermodel is still a body capable of odors, errant hairs, puss, bile, diarrhea, snot, wrinkles, and vomit. Following this logic, all beauty can be a baited trap, because all bodies are capable of malfunctioning.[17]

This avatar alarm can be spotted in the blockbuster novel *Ready Player One*. In it, the protagonist, Wade, splits his time between the real world and a virtual one called OASIS. When he describes his love interest Art3mis, he lingers on her authenticity:

> In the OASIS, you got used to seeing freakishly beautiful faces on everyone. But Art3mis's features didn't look as though they'd been selected from a beauty drop-down menu on some avatar creation template. Her face had the distinctive look of a real person's, as if her true features had been scanned in and mapped onto her avatar. Big hazel eyes, rounded cheekbones, a pointy chin, and a perpetual smirk."

This realness made her "unbearably attractive."[18]

Art3mis's face and body ("Short and Rubenesque. All curves.") stands in direct contrast to the other female players, whom Wade finds fake. "In the OASIS, you usually saw one of two body shapes on female avatars: the absurdly thin yet wildly popular supermodel frame, or the top-heavy, wasp-waisted porn starlet physique."[19] (The fact that none of these female players want to be a T. Rex or a Pegasus or a Pikachu in a world where anything is possible speaks to the fact that the patriarchy's beauty standards are hardcoded into any gathering point.) Art3mis is seen as superior because unlike the other female players in this world, she has an authentic body, an authentic avatar. And it's a desirable one.

However, during their flirtation, one of Wade's primary concerns is that Art3mis could be physically misrepresenting herself. In several severely transphobic passages, he obsesses that Art3mis could be "some 300 lb. dude named Chuck who lives in his mother's basement in suburban Detroit." At one point, he interrogates her via chat. "Now, spill it. Are you a woman? And by that I mean are you a human female who has never had a sex-change operation?"[20]

When at last he finds her photo, Wade has to take a deep breath to steady himself before looking at it. He's relieved to find, "she looked almost identical to her avatar. The same dark hair, the same hazel eyes, and the same beautiful face I knew so well." The only difference between the real self and the virtual is a port-wine stain birthmark, a "flaw" that Wade finds charming and lovable, adding a dose of good white guy saviorism to his romance. "To my eyes, the birthmark did absolutely nothing to diminish her beauty. If anything, the face I saw in the photo seemed even more beautiful to me."[21] Even in a video game fantasy world with robot battles and space castles, women must adhere to their avatars or be considered immoral, a disappointment, or both.

I suppose Wade could be applauded for his attraction to Rubenesque women with port-wine stain birthmarks, which do fall outside Western society's extremely limited definition of what's considered "conventionally attractive." (Though I'd argue that being enthralled by a fleshy, sword-slinging chick with a birthmark is a very low bar to clear. Wade is the dystopian future's "curvy wife guy.") But obviously, there's a reason the female avatars on OASIS come from the supermodel or porn-star template. To start, author Ernest Cline is recreating his own white male gaze in this novel. He refused to adjust his perspective, or couldn't imagine a realm where this wasn't the norm. And it is very much the norm. Girls have been taught since early childhood the rewards of presenting as the fashion doll or the sex doll, and those rewards are the same in digital spaces. If conforming to your avatar means showing your flaws, you risk a disadvantage, especially when others can level-up and award themselves physical perfection with a few button taps.

Zimmerman jokingly writes that molding your body to fit ideals becomes an impossible task because the ultimate beauty ideal is for a "body to disappear entirely and be replaced with an airbrushed photo that can still do sex."[22] I would agree, but I would say this end game isn't a punchline. In this new arena, there will be only one way to advance: Internalize the avatar.

* * *

This would not be the first time women have absorbed and internalized a tool used to distort appearance. Consider the corset. Often the image we have of the corset is pure comedy:

The society woman desperately clutching a bedpost while her maid violently yanks on her lacing, perhaps putting a boot on the lady's backside for leverage. But corsets weren't limited to the vain or the monied. Even working-class women wore them because, as fashion historian Valerie Steele puts it, "comfort has always been less important than female beauty, social status, and respectability." The tradeoff—shallow breathing for a cinched waist—was considered a fair one. The disappearance of the corset can be seen as a sign of progress: At last, women can move and breathe freely! But did the corset ever really leave? Not according to many scholars, including Steele. "Women have internalized the corset through diet and exercise," she says. "They go to the YMCA for body sculpting classes and instead of lacing up, they do hundreds of ab exercises."[23] In other words, the corset and its discomfort is still with us. We've simply shifted the breathless effort from bone casing to bicycle crunches.

Likewise, the avatar is shifting off screen onto the body. In the last ten years, there has been an escalation of exaggerated contoured makeup and social media filters. This level of visual manipulation used to be reserved for professional photoshoots, but now it has reset a new normal. I see a future where there is a singularity between the split-screen of the avatar and the self. Imagine wearable collars that project light and shadow, or color, onto your face, giving you a "filter" for the physical world. Or an invisible polymer film you can wear on your skin that erases imperfections and adds pigment. I am not describing a *Ready Player One*-type dystopian future.

This "Second Skin" film already exists, created by scientists at Harvard and MIT, moving us toward a time where we select and apply the face we show to the world, one that's poreless, hairless, wrinkle-free—no longer even skin but a surface as glossy and slick as an iPhone. For the unaltered face, it is truly game over.

*　*　*

My own Bitmoji was a short-lived phase. A fad. Like many dolls, I played with her for a moment and then outgrew her. Years later, the 2020 pandemic hit, and my entire life, both work and social, moved onto Zoom. The video resolution on my laptop erased any fine lines, and the LED light I bought for my office flattened the shadows on my face. Then Zoom introduced Snapchat-like filters that added rosy cheeks and sparkling cartoon eyes. Through these transformations, I realized I had become my Bitmoji. During that year, she was the one that attended my happy-hour drinks, book readings, and Netflix watch parties, all within a virtual space. In my masked, quarantined life, she became my only public face.

After a lifetime of failing to perfectly mirror my dolls— the Barbies, the porcelain dolls, the American Girl Dolls, the Audrey Hepburn doll—I had finally reached the end goal I'd been coached to achieve since the very beginning: I had become a doll.

And all it cost me was the physical reality of everything and everyone in my former life.

CONCLUSION

It's 1985, and I'm in a Seattle toy store with my older brother, Juan, and my mother. It's a little neighborhood boutique in a suburban shopping "village" not far from school with the unfortunate name of Mr. Peeper's. The shop is no bigger than our living room, overcrowded with Gund stuffed animals and jewel-like rock candy in glass jars. My brother wants to buy a pocket-size baby doll with his allowance. It's a little plastic infant with molded hair and blue-and-white striped pajamas held on by snap buttons. But he understands as a boy, he's not supposed to make this purchase. I watch him pacing around the back of the shop, embarrassed to take the doll to the register. After a whispered consultation with my mother, he pushes money into her hand then ducks out to the parking lot. A little bell above the door chimes as he speeds off to the car.

"Oh, he's just feeling . . . shy about this," my mother tells me sotto voce gazing at the plastic orphaned baby in her hands along with a wad of bills that still bear the imprint of my brother's knuckled grip. She steers us toward the counter where the shopkeeper, a spectacled old granny-type, assesses our pajamed purchase with a nod of approval toward me.

"She picked a cute one!" she pronounces, ringing it up. I hold my breath while she bags it.

Purchase complete, my mother and I walk out of the shop to find my brother leaning against our Honda hatchback, hands jammed in his pockets. Only here does the handoff take place—my mom passes him the bag, like contraband, with the doll inside. We're silent on the drive home.

My brother's interest in this Little Boy Blue was brief. Not long after this covert purchase, he abandoned the doll to go back to *Star Wars* and Hot Wheels and Transformers, sensing that his place was in the realm of space swashbuckling, hot rods, and alien robots. As my brother is just two-and-a-half years older than me, we were playmates, and I often joined him in action-adventure mayhem, playing the Leia to his Luke. Afternoons of "pew-pew" laser guns and "whoosh-whoosh" lightsabers were our mainstay. But unlike my brother, I continued to play with an ocean of dolls—baby dolls, Barbie dolls, paper dolls, collectible dolls, and on and on. These were the toys I'd reach for when playing with a friend, a cousin, or just by myself.

As my only sibling, my brother is the closest I'll get to a twin, and scientific studies often rely on twins because they narrow the variables. In 2016, Scott Kelly returned to Earth after spending 340 days suspended in orbit. Once grounded, Scott was swabbed and poked and scanned, but so was his Earth-bound twin brother, Mark, who acted as a control. Likewise, my brother and I had the same parents, grew up in the same towns, went to the same schools, watched the same

DuckTales cartoons, and ate the same whole-wheat-bread-and-peanut-butter sandwiches. Except I took a voyage to the Planet of the Dolls and spent years floating in a Milky Way of coded feminine stereotypes.

As we grew up, our paths forked in stereotypically gendered ways. I went to a women's college; my brother went to co-ed. I studied humanities; my brother studied physics and astronomy. I went into publishing, a field in which 78 percent of my colleagues self-identify as women; my brother went into STEM academics, a field where 67.6 percent of the higher-ed graduates self-identify as men.[1, 2]

That's not to say we're in lockstep with everything associated with our genders. I love video games, comic books, and Marvel movies. He's generally ambivalent about sports and wears his hair in a long ponytail. Of the two of us, my brother is the one who chose parenthood. But then, even that could be another future dolls foretold. When he tosses his little boy into the air to thrilled squeals and giggles, I see that striped pajama baby he wanted badly enough to break rank with rigid '80s gender norms. My own baby dolls were displaced by fashion dolls and porcelain dolls, so it makes sense I opted out of mothering. I was never much for Velcro diapers, then or now.

At times, I wonder: If my brother had continued playing with dolls and I'd avoided them entirely, would we be in each other's place in terms of our relationships, our careers, our senses of self? If our lives are the outcome of a series of variables, then who can say how much impact the presence or absence of dolls had as a variable in the people we became?

I wish I could submit myself to NASA for a battery of tests and results. I can picture myself on a gurney surrounded by ultra-official-looking people in white lab coats. Their clipboards hold a list of tick-marked changes. If only a blood draw could show a calculable drop in self-esteem or a brain scan could demonstrate the absorption of negative stereotypes. If only we could measure these things the way NASA measures the bone and muscle deterioration of astronauts.

And yet, even with the downsides, I'm reluctant to turn my back on my beloved dolls. Yes, with all the criticism I've logged on these pages, would it surprise you to learn that I still love these frilly, girlie playthings? As culture writer Isabelia Herrera once said in a *New York Times* roundtable, "Critique, for me, has to be an act of love—or else it's a waste of time." So, all my frustration, my complaints, are a way of pushing for change in something that remains dear to me, and to many children.

After all, what would my life have been like without my rocket ship voyage through the fantastical ruffled, sequined, bowed galaxy of dolls? What did my brother miss out on, not just with the Mr. Peeper's doll, but with the seductive Barbies, the progressive Kewpie dolls, the time-traveling American Girls, the Hollywood-bound celebs? What delights did he miss? What book might he have written? I paid an immeasurable price for my trip, but he also paid a price by staying behind, for being denied this universe of femininity. That is yet another loss that cannot be measured.

Like the closing credits of a movie, I picture the camera panning back to show that our story—the story of two children becoming adults surrounded by the gender guardrails of our toys—is the story of everyone who grows up with toys from a commercial industry. Toys that, as we play with them, play us too. Which leaves me with one final, larger question: Who would we be as a society if dolls didn't dictate the outcome first?

ACKNOWLEDGMENTS

My first thanks must go to my trio of Object Lessons editors—Christopher Schaberg, Ian Bogost, Haaris Naqvi—three men who not only saw the merit in exploring something as girlish as dolls but championed it as a topic of deep intellectual exploration. Ian was an advocate of my other women-focused essays in *The Atlantic,* and Christopher pushed me to make this manuscript more "extra"—a note I'll always take. Emily Livingston also added her insight, and the entire team at Bloomsbury—production, art, marketing, and others—have my gratitude for supporting this book with their talents.

I cannot thank Brian Gresko enough for his feedback at every stage of this book. He is a born teacher and motivator—and it shows. I also have to thank my wonderful writing community at the Twenty-Third Street Salon (Court Stroud, Edward Sarfaty, Lisa L. Kirchner, Dorri Olds, Alex Miller, Betsy Farber, Jeff Henigson, Johanna Berkman, Sheila McClear, Laura Sharp, Emillio Mesa, Michael Crawford, Sarah Doneghy, and others) who gave feedback on this text and have supported me through every phase in my writing career. To my writing mentor, Francis Flaherty, thank you for cheering on my writing efforts and giving me the confidence to keep submitting in the face of rejection. I treasure our correspondence. And thanks to Susan Shapiro, the great connector, who brought so many of these people into my life.

Another heartfelt thank you to *Atlantic* editor Lenika Cruz for taking a chance on me at the beginning of my career when I was an unknown writer in her inbox with no big bylines to lend me cache. And it follows that I also have to thank superstar writer Luke Epplin, who was so generous with his editorial contacts and showed me a writing career I wanted to emulate.

I've also been lucky enough to work among many passionate wordsmiths in my day jobs, especially in my time at Fodor's Travel, Oyster, and SmarterTravel Media. I am beyond blessed to have been in these communities where the written word was treated with reverence and writing ambition was applauded. I must give a special shout-out to Josh Roberts, a member of the 5-AM writing squad, who showed me that it was possible to pursue fulfilling writing in your off hours, even if you're a bit sleep deprived. Also hats off to Kelsey Blodget, another shining example of writing with heart in whatever time you have to spare. I also have to extend a thank you to Rachel Klein, who has always offered good counsel in reply to my every text and phone call.

My support system would be incomplete without my family, including my in-laws Tom and Rosemary, who have read and signal-boosted all my articles. I wish every writer could be so lucky. The extended Hart clan has rallied around my efforts. And the Burwells have always been in my corner as well, even popping up in my essays. I also want to thank my family in Chile, who have made me who I am in so many ways. I would be remiss if I didn't include the Winters as well.

All my thanks to my parents, who raised me with a love of antiquing and combing through junk piles. My father always encouraged me to write a book. He would have been proud to put this on his shelf. And my mother was my doll co-conspirator from the jump, indulging my endless treasure hunts. Her encouragement of my eccentric hobby was the starting point of this book.

I also want to extend love to my nieces and nephews—Erin, Will, Annika, and Simoncito—watching you play has informed this book and brightened my life.

Thank you to Mickey Lambert and Nina Callaway, who encouraged me to run toward this project even though fear had me rooted to the spot. Nina especially, my sister through everything in life, has gone above and beyond in her support. Her wall of mint-condition Barbie dolls is evidence that what she loves, she loves with all her heart, and I am lucky to be a recipient of her megawatt light. And finally, all my love and thanks to David Hart, who despite being thoroughly creeped out by dolls, insisted I write this book and dive into months of research with source material that spooked the bejesus out of him. Thankfully, his love of me remains unshaken, and I am eternally grateful.

NOTES

Introduction

1 "Oh, You Beautiful Doll," Nat D. Ayer (music), Seymour Brown (words), 1911 Victor performed by Billy Murray and The American Quartet.

2 Deborah Thompson, "At Home with Richard Simmons," *Doll Reader,* May 1998.

3 Trixie Mattel, "Trixie's Decades of Dolls: The '90s." YouTube video. May 7, 2020. https://www.youtube.com/watch?v=UrJh4 -fF4RE&t=510s.

4 "William's Doll," Mary Rodgers (music), Sheldon Harnick (words), November 1972, Media Sound Studios and CBS Studios, performed by Alan Alda and Marlo Thomas.

5 Jacey Fortin, "Transgender Doll Based on Jazz Jennings to Debut in New York," *New York Times,* February 17, 2017, ƒhttps://www.nytimes.com/2017/02/17/business/transgender -doll-jazz-jennings.html.

6 Eliana Dockterman, "'A Doll for Everyone': Meet Mattel's Gender-Neutral Doll," *Time,* September 25, 2019 https://time .com/5684822/mattel-gender-neutral-doll/.

7 Alex Myers, "The Alarming Message of Mattel's 'Gender-Neutral' Dolls," *Slate,* November 8, 2019, https://slate.com/

business/2019/11/mattel-gender-neutral-dolls-are-about-sales
.html.

8 Trixie Mattel, "Trixie's Decades of Dolls: The '80s." YouTube
video. April 30, 2020. https://www.youtube.com/watch?v
=FD43vZrPoGo.

Chapter 1

1 David M. Ewalt, "A Real Doll," *Forbes,* March 5, 2009, https://
www.forbes.com/2009/03/05/real-barbie-proportions
-business_distortion.html?sh=230a90e041ba.

2 Jillian Steinhauer, "Deconstructing Barbie's Disproportion,"
Hyperallergic, July 5, 2013, https://hyperallergic.com/74913/
deconstructing-barbies-disproportion/.

3 Gene Kim and Benji Jones, "We compared our bodies
to Barbie. Here's what the doll would look like in read
life," *Insider,* January 2, 2021 (updated), https://www
.businessinsider.com/barbie-ken-dolls-would-look-like-real
-life-unrealistic-body-2019-6.

4 "Feminists Protest 'Sexist' Toys in Fair," *New York Times,*
February 29, 1972, https://www.nytimes.com/1972/02/29/
archives/feminists-protest-sexist-toys-in-fair.html.

5 Tanya Lee Stone, *The Good, The Bad, and the Barbie: A Doll's
History and Her Impact on Us,* (Viking Book for Young
Readers, 2010), 57.

6 Hole, "Doll Parts," 1994.

7 Hole, "Doll Parts," Youtube video. https://www.youtube.com/
watch?v=RD9xK9smth4.

8   Madeline Boardman, "Courtney Love Doesn't Regret Her Nose Job, Lost Acting Role to Julia Roberts in Satisfaction," *US Weekly,* November 19, 2014, https://www.usmagazine.com/celebrity-news/news/courtney-love-doesnt-regret-nose-job-lost-movie-gig-to-julie-roberts-20141911/.

9   Charlotte Cowles, "Courtney Love's Fresh Start," *Harper's Bazaar,* July 14, 2015, https://www.harpersbazaar.com/culture/features/a11467/courtney-love-0815/.

10   Stone, *The Good, The Bad, and the Barbie: A Doll's History and Her Impact on Us,* 32.

11   Ann Shoket, *Seventeen Ultimate Guide to Guys: What He Really Thinks About Flirting, Dating, Relationships, and YOU!,* (Running Press Adult, 2013), 12.

12   Rebecca Flood, "Living Doll: UK's oldest real-life Barbie, 48, who's spent 32k pounds on 105 surgeries in 13 years now gets a new face," *The Sun,* June 10, 2019, https://www.thesun.co.uk/fabulous/9260457/old-human-barbie-doll-face-surgery-plastic/.

13   Marianne Mychaskiw, "Welcome to the Dollhouse; A Conversation With Human Barbie, Nannette Hammond," *InStyle,* March 13, 2017 (updated), https://www.instyle.com/beauty/nannette-hammond-human-barbie-interview.

14   Aqua, "Barbie Girl," *Aquarium,* 1997.

15   Michael Idov, "This Is Not a Barbie Doll. This Is an Actual Human Being," *GQ,* July 12, 2017, https://www.gq.com/story/valeria-lukyanova-human-barbie-doll.

16   "THE FIRST WE GIRLS CAN DO ANYTHING BARBIE SLOGAN COMMERCIAL." YouTube video. Posted by 80scommercialsforever, August 15, 2009, https://www.youtube.com/watch?v=CXVFrHwXHwA.

17 Tanya Lee Stone, *The Good, The Bad, and the Barbie: A Doll's History and Her Impact on Us,* (Viking Book for Young Readers, 2010), 85.

18 Tracie Egan Morrissey, "Growing Up, Everyone Did Dirty Things With Their Barbies," *Jezebel*, September 12, 2007, https://jezebel.com/growing-up-everyone-did-dirty-things-with-their-barbie-299195.

19 Anthony Ferguson, "The Sex Doll: A History," (McFarland & Company, 2010), 27–29.

20 Julie Beck, "A (Straight, Male) History of Sex Dolls," *The Atlantic*, August 6, 2014, https://www.theatlantic.com/health/archive/2014/08/a-straight-male-history-of-dolls/375623/.

21 *Ex Machina,* 2014, directed and written by Alex Garland.

22 Amy Kurzweil, "(Me)chanical Reproduction, Technofeelia vol.13," *The Believer,* December 2020/January 2021.

23 Ta-Nehisi Coates, "What We Mean When We Say 'Race Is a Social Construct,'" *The Atlantic*, May 15, 2013, https://www.theatlantic.com/national/archive/2013/05/what-we-mean-when-we-say-race-is-a-social-construct/275872/.

24 Kelly Kasulis, "Asian Barbie's evolution wasn't intelligently designed," February 14, 2016, https://www.bostonglobe.com/ideas/2016/02/14/asian-barbie-evolution-wasn-intelligently-designed/ILEA5pNcGUGBVpUZwrpHMK/story.html.

25 Koa Beck, *White Feminism: From the Suffragettes to Influencers and Who They Leave Behind*, (Atria Books, 2021), 22.

26 Hillary Crosley, "Nicki Minaj Explains the Origin of Her 'Barbies,'" *MTV News*, October 29, 2010, http://www.mtv.com/news/2494471/nicki-minaj-rapfix-live-barbie/.

27 Orly Lobel, *You Don't Own Me: How Mattel v. MGA Entertainment Exposed Barbie's Dark Side,* (W.W. Norton & Company, 2017), 34–52.

28 Mitchell Sunderland, "Meet the Designers Behind the Controversial Bratz Dolls," *Vice,* January 26, 2016, https://www.vice.com/en/article/qkgyvx/meet-the-designers-behind-the-controversial-bratz-dolls.

29 Arnold Veraa, PhD, "Critique: Report of the APA Task Force on the Sexualization of Girls (2007)," The Institute for Psychological Therapies, Volume 18, 2009, http://www.ipt-forensics.com/journal/volume18/j18_2.htm.

30 "Weekend Update: Barbie on Her 50th Birthday – SNL," *Saturday Night Live,* https://www.youtube.com/watch?v=wDkjI7YMNbg&t=77s.

31 Mitchell Sunderland, "Meet the Designers Behind the Controversial Bratz Dolls," *Vice,* January 26, 2016, https://www.vice.com/en/article/qkgyvx/meet-the-designers-behind-the-controversial-bratz-dolls.

32 Jonita Davis, "A study found adults see black girls as 'less innocent,' shocking everyone but black moms," *The Washington Post,* July 13, 2017, https://www.washingtonpost.com/news/parenting/wp/2017/07/13/a-study-found-adults-see-black-girls-as-less-innocent-shocking-everyone-but-black-moms/.

33 Andy Golder, "Bratz—The Toy Company—Made A Really Good Statement About Racism And Social Justice," *Buzzfeed*, May 31, 2020, https://www.buzzfeed.com/andyneuenschwander/bratz-anti-racist-message-black-lives-matter.

34 Ibid.

35 Jamie Samhan, "Mattel's Barbie To 'Increase Black Representation' And 'Spotlight More Black Role Models,'" *ET Canada*, June 12, 2020, https://etcanada.com/news/656287/mattels-barbie-to-increase-black-representation-and-spotlight-more-black-role-models/.

36 Morgan Sung, "Barbie, the only good YouTuber, explains racism in her latest vlog," *Mashable*, October 8, 2020, https://mashable.com/article/barbie-explains-racism-vlog/.

37 Toni Morrison, "It's like growing up black one more time," *New York Times*, August 11, 1974, https://www.nytimes.com/1974/08/11/archives/rediscovering-black-history-it-is-like-growing-up-black-one-more.html.

38 "Barbie had best sales in more than five year in lockdown boost," *BBC News*, February 9, 2020, https://www.bbc.com/news/business-56004366.

Chapter 2

1 Theresa Oneill, *Ungovernable: The Victorian Parent's Guide to Raising Flawless Children,* (Little, Brown and Company, 2019), 132.

2 Hugh Cunningham, *Children and Childhood in Western Society since 1500,* (Longman, 1995), 62–42.

3 Miriam Formanek-Brunell, *Made to Play House: Dolls and the Commercialization of American Girlhood, 1830-1930,* (Yale University, 1993), 7.

4 Cunningham, *Children and Childhood in Western Society since 1500,*138.

5 Formanek-Brunell, *Made to Play House: Dolls and the Commercialization of American Girlhood,* 3.

6   Ibid, 16.

7   Antonia Fraser, *Dolls,* (Octopus Books Limited, 1963), 35.

8   Manfred Bachmann and Claus Hansmann, *Dolls the Wide World Over*, (Crown Publishers, Inc., 1971), 40.

9   Gary Cross, *Kids' Stuff: Toys and the Changing World of American Childhood,* (Harvard University Press, 1997), 43.

10   Thessaly La Force, "The European Obsession With Porcelain," *New Yorker,* November 11, 2015, https://www.newyorker.com/books/page-turner/the-european-obsession-with-porcelain.

11   Ibid.

12   Antonia Fraser, *Dolls,* (Octopus Books Limited, 1963), 27.

13   Ibid, 65–70.

14   Formanek-Brunell, *Made to Play House: Dolls and the Commercialization of American Girlhood*, 13.

15   Ibid, 16–18.

16   Ibid, 20–23.

17   Ibid, 20–23.

18   Emma Tarlo, "The Secret History of Buying and Selling Hair," *Smithsonian Magazine,* November 14, 2016, https://www.smithsonianmag.com/history/secret-history-buying-and-selling-hair-180961080/.

19   Linda Rodriguez McRobbie, "The History of Creepy Dolls," *Smithsonian Magazine,* July 15, 2015, https://www.smithsonianmag.com/history/history-creepy-dolls-180955916/.

20   Reynale Smith Pickering, "The New Christmas Doll Complains," *The Ladies Home Journal,* December 1908.

21   Robin Bernstein, Racial Innocence: Performing American Childhood from Slavery to Civil Rights, (New York University Press, 2011), 17.

22 Jon Henley, "From bedtime story to ugly insult: how Victorian caricature became a racist slur," *The Guardian*, February 5, 2009, https://www.theguardian.com/media/2009/feb/06/race-thatcher-golliwog.

23 Robin Bernstein, Racial Innocence: Performing American Childhood from Slavery to Civil Rights, (New York University Press, 2011), 18.

24 Julian K. Jarboe, "The Racial Symbolism of the Topsy-Turvy Doll." *The Atlantic*, November 2015, https://www.theatlantic.com/technology/archive/2015/11/the-racial-symbolism-of-the-topsy-turvy-doll/416985/.

25 Robin Bernstein, *Racial Innocence: Performing American Childhood from Slavery to Civil Rights*, (New York University Press, 2011), 16.

26 Leila McNeill, "How a Psychologist's Work on Race Identity Helped Overturn School Segregation in 1950s America," *Smithsonian Magazine*, October 26, 2017, https://www.smithsonianmag.com/science-nature/psychologist-work-racial-identity-helped-overturn-school-segregation-180966934/.

27 Theresa Oneill, *Ungovernable: The Victorian Parent's Guide to Raising Flawless Children*, (Little, Brown and Company, 2019), 151.

28 "Dolly Dear," Child Labor Builletin, August 1913, Also see Formanek-Brunell, *Made to Play House: Dolls and the Commercialization of American Girlhood, 1830-1930*, 114–115.

29 Shelley Armitage, *Kewpies and Beyond: The World of Rose O'Neill*, (University Press of Mississippi, 1994), 6.

30 Ibid, ix.

31 Ibid, 120.

32 Stephanie Buck, "Meet the hardcore feminist who created the cute Kewpie doll," *Timeline*, November 8, 2016, https://timeline.com/kewpie-doll-rose-oneill-480de6506035

Chapter 3

1 Antonia Fraser, *Dolls,* (Octopus Books Limited, 1963), 6.

2 Manfred Bachmann and Claus Hansmann, *Dolls the Wide World Over*, (Crown Publishers, Inc., 1971), 19.

3 *American Girls* podcast, "Looking for a Hero: Felicity Saves the Day," April 15, 2019.

4 Henry Wiencek, "The Dark Side of Thomas Jefferson," *Smithsonian Magazine,* October 2012, https://www.smithsonianmag.com/history/the-dark-side-of-thomas-jefferson-35976004/.

5 Felicia R. Lee "Harvesting Cotton-Field Capitalism," *New York Times*, October 3, 2014, https://www.nytimes.com/2014/10/04/books/the-half-has-never-been-told-follows-the-money-of-slavery.html.

6 "The Beginning of Forever | @American Girl" YouTube video, Posted by American Girl, May 15, 2014, https://youtu.be/fAhd7-p0eDs.

7 Julia Rubin, "All Dolled Up: The Enduring Triumph of American Girl," *Racked*, June 29, 2015, https://www.racked.com/2015/6/29/8855683/american-girl-doll-store.

8 Dana Goldstein, "Two States. Eight Textbooks, Two American Stories," *New York Times,* January 12, 2020, https://www

.nytimes.com/interactive/2020/01/12/us/texas-vs-california -history-textbooks.html.

9   "The Beginning of Forever | @American Girl" American Girl, https://youtu.be/fAhd7-p0eDs.

10 Lisa W. Foderaro, "Doll's Village: Some See Restoration as Too Cutesy," *New York Times,* December 7, 2007, https://www .nytimes.com/2007/12/07/nyregion/07doll.html.

11 Aisha Harris, "The Making of an American Girl," *Slate*, September 21, 2006, https://slate.com/culture/2016/09/the -making-of-addy-walker-american-girls-first-black-doll.html.

12 @Goaldiggin_D1va. "I'm just now realizing that "American Girl" hustled me to buy a slave doll!!! Why was the only Black American Girl a legit Slave!!!! I legit BEGGED my parents for that doll, and she came with a cotton dress and a feather bed. Man smh happy #juneteenth #Addy #americangirl." Twitter, June 19, 2019, 8:00p.m., https://twitter.com/Goaldiggin_D1va /status/1141541387277492225.

13 @francescalyn. "I think I should sell my Addy American Girl doll. But I feel really weird putting an escaped slave doll up for auction on eBay." Twitter, December 24, 2017, 2:07p.m., https://twitter.com/francescalyn/status /945038316654809089.

14 @TakiyahNAmin. "Calling Addy a "slave doll" is so reductive. What's embedded in that tweet is that she shouldn't have been marketed or sold. Spoken like someone who didn't read the books or know about AG dolls. . .#longliveAddy. I'm with you @ChaniThaHippie on this . . . 🕊 🖤." Twitter, August 30, 2019, 10:15a.m., https://twitter.com/TakiyahNAmin/status /1167485971044192256.

15 Rubin, "All Dolled Up: The Enduring Triumph of American Girl."

16 Emilie Zaslow, *Playing with America's Doll*, (Palgrave, 2017), 179.

17 Marcia Chatelain, "American Historian, Meet American Girl," Historians.org, December 1, 2015, https://www.historians .org/publications-and-directories/perspectives-on-history/ december-2015/american-historian-meet-american-girl.

18 Koa Beck, *White Feminism: From the Suffragettes to Influencers and Who They Leave Behind*, (Atria Books, 2021), 39.

19 *American Girls* podcast, "Meet Felicity, Meet Us," February 28, 2019.

20 Emilie Zaslow, *Playing with America's Doll*, (Palgrave, 2017), 92.

21 Rubin, "All Dolled Up: The Enduring Triumph of American Girl."

22 Ibid.

23 Marcia Chatelain, "American Historian, Meet American Girl," Historians.org, December 1, 2015, https://www.historians .org/publications-and-directories/perspectives-on-history/ december-2015/american-historian-meet-american-girl.

24 Alexandra Petri, "Even more terrible things are happening to the American Girl brans than you thought," *The Washington Post*, May 1, 2013, https://www.washingtonpost.com/blogs /compost/wp/2013/05/01/even-more-terrible-things-are -happening-to-the-american-girl-doll-brand-than-you -thought/.

25 Christopher Borrelli, "The American Girl Way," *Chicago Tribune,* December 21, 2011, https://www.chicagotribune.com /entertainment/ct-xpm-2011-12-21-ct-ent-1222-american -girl-20111221-story.html.

26 Meilan Solly, "The Enduring Nostalgia of American Girl Dolls," *Smithsonian*, June 3, 2021, https://www.smithsonianmag.com/history/evolution-american-girl-dolls-180977822/.

27 Elizabeth Minkel, "Why it doesn't matter what Benedict Cumberbatch thinks of Sherlock fan fiction," *The New Statesman*, October 17, 2014, https://www.newstatesman.com/culture/2014/10/why-it-doesn-t-matter-what-benedict-cumberbatch-thinks-sherlock-fan-fiction.

28 *American Girls* podcast, "Felicity Futures Part I—Fan Fiction," May 13, 2019.

29 @PlatypusInPlaid. "The fact that the character Courtney owns an original 1986 Molly doll means that the American Girl Company is canon within the American Girl universe. History has caught up with itself. The cycle is complete. This Ouroboros has swallowed its own tail." Twitter, September 15, 2020, 9:50p.m., https://twitter.com/PlatypusInPlaid/status/1306092958089908224.

Chapter 4

1 Antonia Fraser, *Dolls,* (Octopus Books Limited, 1963), 87.

2 Susan J. Douglas and Andrea McDonnell, *Celebrity: A History of Fame,* (New York University Press, 2019), 72–74.

3 Douglas and McDonnell, *Celebrity: A History of Fame*, 97.

4 Hadley Meares, "The Peculiar History of Celebrity Dolls," *Atlas Obscura*, April 5, 2016, https://www.atlasobscura.com/articles/the-peculiar-history-of-celebrity-dolls.

5 "Shirley Temple Biography," *Biography*, https://www.biography.com/actor/shirley-temple.

6 Gary Cross, *Kids' Stuff: Toys and the Changing World of American Childhood,* (Harvard University Press, 1997), 117.

7 Shirley Temple Black, *Child Star: An Autobiography,* (McGraw-Hill, 1988), 68–69.

8 Susan J. Douglas and Andrea McDonnell, *Celebrity: A History of Fame,* (New York University Press, 2019), 4.

9 Dan Ronan, "The Dionne quintuplets: A Depression-era freak show," *CNN,* November 19, 1997, http://www.cnn.com/US /9711/19/dionne.quints/index.html.

10 Cross, *Kids' Stuff: Toys and the Changing World of American Childhood,* 102–103.

11 Betty Friedan, *The Feminine Mystique,* (W.W. Norton, 1963), 115.

12 Cross, *Kids' Stuff: Toys and the Changing World of American Childhood,* 109.

13 Douglas and McDonnell, *Celebrity: A History of Fame,* 64–65.

14 Robert A. Frahm, "Boys Get More Attention in Class Than Girls, National Study Finds," *Hartford Courant,* February 12, 1992, https://www.courant.com/news/connecticut/hc-xpm -1992-02-12-0000204148-story.html.

15 Bernstein, *Racial Innocence: Performing American Childhood from Slavery to Civil Rights,* 26–28.

16 Tavi Gevinson, "Britney Spears Was Never in Control," *The Cut,* February 23, 2021, https://www.thecut.com/2021/02/ tavi-gevinson-britney-spears-was-never-in-control.html?utm _medium=s1&utm_campaign=thecut&utm_source=tw.

17 Betsy Golden Kellem, "How the Real Madame Tussauds Build a Business Out of Beheadings," *Atlas Obscura,* October 10, 2017, https://www.atlasobscura.com/articles/tussauds.

18 Edward Carey, "Madame Tussaud: the astounding tale of survival behind the woman who made history" *The Guardian,* October 4, 2018, https://amp.theguardian.com/books/2018/oct/04/madame-tussaud-edward-carey-little.

19 Golden Kellem, "How the Real Madame Tussauds Build a Business Out of Beheadings."

20 Carey, "Madame Tussaud: the astounding tale of survival behind the woman who made history."

21 Golden Kellem, "How the Real Madame Tussauds Build a Business Out of Beheadings."

22 Carey, "Madame Tussaud: the astounding tale of survival behind the woman who made history."

23 Golden Kellem, "How the Real Madame Tussauds Build a Business Out of Beheadings."

24 Lia Ryerson, "11 hilariously bad dolls that look nothing like the celebrities they're modeled after," *Insider,* June 10, 2019, https://www.insider.com/celebrity-doll-fails-2018-3.

25 Eleanor Harvie, "16 Celeb Dolls That Are So Bad They Will Make You Cry," *The Talko,* February 22, 2017, https://www.thetalko.com/15-celeb-dolls-that-are-so-bad-they-will-make-you-cry/.

26 You Must Remember This, Karina Longworth, "Dead Blondes, Part 1" through Dead Blondes, Part 13," January 31, 2017-April 25, 2017.

27 *Beginners,* Focus Features, directed by Mike Mills, 2010.

28 Tanya Lee Stone, *The Good, The Bad, and the Barbie: A Doll's History and Her Impact on Us,* (Viking Book for Young Readers, 2010), 88.

29 Ibid, 90.

30 Tracie Egan Morrissey, "Weekend Homework Assignment: Kill Barbie," *Jezebel*, September 7, 2007, https://jezebel.com/weekend-homework-assignment-kill-barbie-297696.

31 Hadley Meares, "The Peculiar History of Celebrity Dolls," *Atlas Obscura*, April 5, 2016, https://www.atlasobscura.com/articles/the-peculiar-history-of-celebrity-dolls.

32 Jia Tolentino, "Athleisure, barre, and kale: the tyranny of the ideal woman," *The Guardian*, August 2, 2019, https://www.theguardian.com/news/2019/aug/02/athleisure-barre-kale-tyranny-ideal-woman-labour.

33 Ibid.

34 Ibid.

Chapter 5

1 "Recap Review: The American Girl Premiere," *Real Women of Gaming*, October 15, 2018, https://realwomenofgaming.com/2018/10/15/__trashed/.

2 Adrienne Raphel, "Our Dolls, Ourselves?" *The New Yorker*, October 9, 2013, https://www.newyorker.com/business/currency/our-dolls-ourselves.

3 Ibid.

4 Amanda Hess, "What Do Our Online Avatars Reveal About Us?" *New York Times Magazine,* May 10, 2016, https://www.nytimes.com/2016/05/15/magazine/what-do-our-online-avatars-reveal-about-us.html.

5 Ian Bogost, "Emoji Don't Mean What They Used To," *The Atlantic,* February 11, 2019, https://www.theatlantic.com/

technology/archive/2019/02/how-new-emoji-are-changing
-pictorial-language/582400/.

6 Hess, "What Do Our Online Avatars Reveal About Us?"

7 Ibid.

8 Laura Parker "Video Games Allow Characters More Varied Sexual Identities," *New York Times,* August 13, 2016, https://www.nytimes.com/2016/09/01/technology/personaltech/video-games-allow-characters-more-varied-sexual-orientations.html.

9 Kellen Browning, "Where Has Your Tween Been During the Pandemic? On This Gaming Site," *New York Times,* August 16, 2020, https://www.nytimes.com/2020/08/16/technology/roblox-tweens-videogame-coronavirus.html.

10 Catherine Gewertz, "Bitmoji Classrooms: Why Teachers Are Buzzing About Them," *Education Week*, July 30, 2020, https://www.edweek.org/teaching-learning/bitmoji-classrooms-why-teachers-are-buzzing-about-them/2020/07.

11 Stephanie Rosenbloom, "It's Love at First Kill," *New York Times,* April 22, 2011, https://www.nytimes.com/2011/04/24/fashion/24avatar.html.

12 Parker "Video Games Allow Characters More Varied Sexual Identities."

13 Hess, "What Do Our Online Avatars Reveal About Us?"

14 Browning, "Where Has Your Tween Been During the Pandemic? On This Gaming Site."

15 Kumari Devarajan, "White Skin, Black Emojis?" *NPR Code Switch*, March 21, 2018, https://www.npr.org/sections/codeswitch/2018/03/21/425573955/white-skin-black-emojis.

16 Jess Zimmerman, *Women and Other Monsters: Building a New Mythology,* (Beacon Press, 2021), 53.

17 Ibid.

18 Ernest Cline, *Ready Player One,* (Ballantine Books, 2011), 35.

19 Ibid.

20 Ibid, 173.

21 Ibid, 376.

22 Zimmerman, *Women and Other Monsters: Building a New Mythology*, 63.

23 Booth Moore, "Waiting to Exhale," *Los Angeles Times,* February 6, 2000, https://www.latimes.com/archives/la-xpm -2000-feb-06-cl-61461-story.html.

Conclusion

1 Lee and Low Books, "Where Is the Diversity in Publishing? The 2019 Diversity Baseline Survey Results," January 28, 2020, https://blog.leeandlow.com/2020/01/28/2019diversitybaseli nesurvey/.

2 USA Facts, "How many women graduates with STEM degrees?" September 28, 2020, https://usafacts.org/articles/ women-stem-degrees/.

INDEX